RUSS ALAN PRINCE ✚ HANNAH SHAW GROVE

BEYOND
PERFORMANCE

*How Hedge Funds Can
Strengthen and Build
Their Affluent Client Base*

SPONSORED BY:
Rothstein Kass

To Konnie and Rob for keeping
the compound running smoothly

» RUSS

For all-weather friendship, to KAO

« HANNAH

TABLE OF
CONTENTS

FOREWORD

HOWARD ALTMAN
Co-Managing Principal, Rothstein Kass

 Hedge funds, widely recognized for their ability to provide superior returns, have rarely been known for their sophisticated marketing approaches. Not long ago, wealthy investors, enticed by the performance of high-profile firms, would compete to invest in new and existing funds before they closed to new investors. Despite media scrutiny and a few notable failures, the promise of greater returns has continued to attract assets to the space at a remarkable pace. In recent years, the industry has grown in terms of the number of firms, products, investors and assets under management. While the net impact of this growth has been overwhelmingly positive, firms will need to take a more strategic approach to franchise development in the intensely competitive marketplace that is emerging.

As trusted advisors to the hedge fund community, we at Rothstein Kass have watched this unfold with great interest to understand the potential impact to our clients and our business. While it is obvious that performance will remain the most important deciding factor in evaluating funds, it is clear that investors are also looking beyond alpha to the franchise value and the less tangible elements of a firm's capabilities.

Beyond Performance: How Hedge Funds Can Strengthen and Build Their Affluent Client Base by Russ Alan Prince and Hannah Shaw Grove examines this trend in greater detail to better understand how hedge funds can be bolstered by a more diligent approach to non-investment activities. As leading authorities on private wealth and high-net worth issues, their research, including interviews with over 400 investors, represents the most extensive and comprehensive evaluation of hedge fund investors ever.

In recent years there have been unprecedented opportunities for hedge funds. This expansion has increased the number of funds available to accredited investors and drawn the interest of institutional investors to the money management talent and strategy of the sector. Yet new challenges will arise. For example, the proliferation of funds with wide-ranging strategies has required firms to expand marketing efforts in areas and ways not seen before. One challenge is that distinct market segments apply their own standards in choosing funds for investment, making targeting difficult. While funds with consistent records of impressive returns typically maintain an advantage over their peers, this benefit can be forfeited or blunted by unclear objectives or poor communication with clients.

Hedge fund assets still represent a small portion of total allocations among accredited and institutional investors. The inflow of assets into this investment class is expected to increase in the near-term, as many economists are predicting prolonged volatility in equity markets. As firms position themselves for the next wave of capital, they should be thinking more than ever about the brand image they project. They will also need to broaden their networks to reflect an industry that relies less on word-of-mouth referrals and more on proactive business development and retention.

The pages that follow examine the scope of the marketing issues facing the industry and outline steps that firms can take to improve their competitive positioning. From sections on segmenting investment populations to client satisfaction efforts, *Beyond Performance* is an entertaining and insightful work featuring actionable advice for all industry participants.

ABOUT
THIS BOOK

For years, the formula for success in the hedge fund industry was simple and straightforward: open a fund and wait for the money to roll in. Indeed, with the relatively small number of funds and some good performance numbers, many investors were clamoring for a piece of the action.

Today, powered by the outsized profits – and the profit potential – the number of hedge funds, and funds-of-funds, has increased exponentially, as has the level of institutional involvement and ownership. As a result, fund firms can no longer count on getting all of the investors, and money, they want simply by opening a new fund. And they can no longer assume the investors who do invest will stay on board if returns falter. In short, hedge funds and funds-of-funds firms now have to work to find – and keep – investors as never before.

To see how fund firms could best address that sea change in the business, we conducted the first and largest survey ever of affluent hedge fund and fund-of-funds investors, 428 people representing aggregate investment assets of $18 billion. Each had an average of 3.3 such funds and a mean investment of $42.1 million. From an investment standpoint, these are exactly the people fund firms want on board. We further subdivided these respondents into demographic and behavioral segments – and then the real work began. How did those affluent investors choose the funds they invested in? On whose advice? What were their expectations? Were those expectations being met? How often were they moving their money, and why?

The results of our study, presented in this book, are revealing. Almost one-third of the respondents, for example, were dissatisfied with their fund firm – and the percentages often rose when the respondents were segmented by demographic or behavioral factors. Furthermore, nearly one in five investors had taken his or her money out of a fund in the previous year. One might surmise that as the number of available funds continues to increase – as the number of investment options proliferates – these figures will rise as well.

Consequently, hedge fund and fund-of-funds firms now have to pay attention to business disciplines that they have, historically, seldom been bothered with: marketing and client service. And this book was written to help fund firms do just that. By better knowing their affluent clients, fund firms can develop strategies and tactics that help them succeed in what is a much more competitive environment, landing, and holding onto, the high-end investors they need and want.

THE ROLE OF
MARKETING

The hedge fund business is booming and, given the amount of money being invested by the affluent in their search for alpha, there's every reason to believe that it will continue to boom for some time. For most hedge fund professionals, running money is a way for them to challenge themselves and exert their intellectual prowess. At the same time, we cannot forget that managing a successful hedge fund or fund-of-funds is one of the very best ways to get wealthy – very, very wealthy. And, it's legal.

The financial and personal rewards of managing money at this level have not, of course, gone unnoticed – they have attracted a lot of press – and a lot of competition. A decade ago, there were far fewer hedge funds and funds-of-funds around and many affluent investors found themselves unable to buy into the top funds, no matter how much they were willing to pay. That is no longer the case; today, so many new competitors have entered the hedge fund and fund-of-funds market that the balance of power has shifted. More than at any other time in the history of these funds, firms have to go out and win the business of the very affluent before they invest somewhere else.

Consequently, a critical factor in the financial success of many hedge fund and fund-of-funds firms is not only their ability to raise money and hold onto it even when their performance dips, but their ability to use segmented marketing to attract and retain affluent investors.

3

SALES VERSUS
MARKETING

For all of that, the hedge fund business is, first and foremost, all about investment performance. If you can deliver sensational numbers and the "right" people know it, then marketing will likely be of limited value to your firm. On the other hand, if you have a newly opened fund or if you don't have a track record that absolutely dazzles (the chicken and egg problem), then marketing can prove to be very useful, if not essential. Even for more established funds that have not yet reached capacity, marketing can be effective in bringing in new affluent investors and even keeping them when performance is off.

The only problem is that, in the hedge fund business, there's not always a clear line between sales and marketing. For instance, when hedge fund managers say they've hired marketing people, as often as not they've really hired sales people whose job it is to bring in money, often based on their personal network, not their marketing expertise.

In working with hedge funds and funds-of-funds on marketing initiatives we have found that it's common for sales people to have little or nothing to offer once they have run through their network of prospective affluent investors. In one survey of 68 marketing professionals working for hedge funds, 76.4 percent reported that within one year they had "tapped out" their network of affluent investors (Exhibit 1.1). This doesn't mean that the marketers could not expand their network, but for many of them, their ability to access new affluent investors becomes severely limited.

EXHIBIT 1.1:

MARKETERS TAP OUT WITHIN A YEAR

N = 68 HEDGE FUND MARKETERS

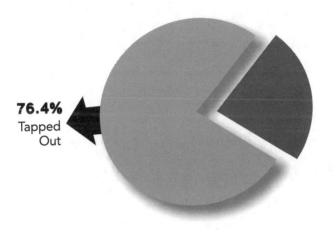

76.4%
Tapped
Out

5

MARKETING
WRIT LARGE

That's where networking ends and marketing begins. And marketing as we define it can be broadly conceptualized as having three components:

COMPONENT #1: Sourcing the Potential Affluent Investor;

COMPONENT #2: Converting the Potential to Actual; and

COMPONENT #3: Managing Client Experiences and Expectations.

COMPONENT #1:

SOURCING THE POTENTIAL AFFLUENT INVESTOR

The appropriateness of hedge funds and funds-of-funds are limited. That is, they're only suitable for a relatively small number of investors. From the affluent to the institutional, such funds are not the normative investment. Moreover, even among these suitable investors, hedge funds and funds-of-funds tend to represent a small (if growing) portion of their allocations. As we see it,

> Marketing is about finding those appropriate investors who are motivated to listen to you "explain" your hedge fund or fund-of-funds.

We will address Component #1 in *Chapter 3: Sourcing Affluent Investors.*

COMPONENT #2:

CONVERTING THE POTENTIAL TO ACTUAL

We've seen quite a number of hedge fund and fund-of-funds professionals pitch their products to affluent investors, family office executives, financial advisors, and pension executives. The methodology employed by many of these professionals in attempting to sell their funds transforms their efforts into a numbers game, but not performance numbers. The sheer volume of potential investors they have to see in order to make one sale is often hugely disproportionate. Therefore,

> Effective marketing is about qualifying a potential investor and customizing the presentation to that investor to dramatically increase your closing ratio.

We will address Component #2 in *Chapter 4: Selecting Hedge Funds and Funds-of-Funds.*

COMPONENT #3:

MANAGING CLIENT EXPERIENCES AND EXPECTATIONS

Unless your performance is unerringly exceptional, managing affluent investor experiences and expectations can provide you with a window of opportunity to offset poor investment performance. Even so, we are talking about a relatively short grace period during which time you will need to get back on track and deliver the goods. As such,

> Marketing is about how to efficaciously manage an investor's experience and expectations, thereby providing you with an all-important grace period when you need it.

We will address Component #3 in *Chapter 5: Switching Behavior* and *Chapter 6: The Importance of Satisfaction.*

7

SEGMENTATION

An underlying precept to successful marketing is the recognition that not all investors are alike. The hedge fund industry tends to discern between taxable and non-taxable investors, but that's usually as far as the distinction goes, at least from a marketing standpoint – and that's not far enough for consistent success:

> Effective marketing is about gaining an in-depth understanding of the behavioral and decision-making processes of investors and incorporating that understanding into the strategies and tactics in Components #1, #2 & #3.

Before examining the various components of marketing, however, we need to understand the key affluent investor segments that invest in hedge funds and funds-of-funds because a tailored approach is key to success at this high level. We will address segmentation in greater detail in the following chapter, *Segmenting Affluent Investors.*

PROFESSIONALIZATION
AND THE NEED FOR MARKETING

There can be no question that, in the hedge fund universe, even the finest marketing is subservient to high-quality investing. Hedge fund professionals bring their talents, their unique abilities, and their specialized skills to the money management industry, and those exceptional capabilities center on portfolio construction, security selection, trading, risk management and other functions that are core to asset management. But the hedge fund industry is quickly moving from adolescence to adulthood, and in the process is increasingly becoming institutionalized. Consequently, we see a growing need and desire by hedge funds to "professionalize" their shops. Marketing – at the sophisticated levels we're talking about here – becomes a meaningful aspect of that "professionalization."

Large, established and sophisticated investors expect a certain degree of infrastructure at the firms they work with, including the functions that can stabilize a product and its assets when the stars don't perfectly align, as might be the case if you are opening a new fund or trying to bounce back from an off-year.

OUR
PERSPECTIVE

Our objective in writing this research-based primer is to provide you with a solid and workable understanding of the keys you can turn to unlock marketing success. The perspectives we're providing come from four sources:

▸▸ The most comprehensive and intensive empirical evaluation of affluent hedge fund and fund-of-funds investors ever conducted – we surveyed 428 affluent hedge fund and fund-of-funds investors with an aggregate investment of US$18 billion.

▸▸ An extensive research study of the financial advisors who direct their affluent clients to hedge funds and funds-of-funds. The financial advisors in this survey invested an average of US$23.8 million per client in hedge funds or funds-of-funds for an average of 6.6 high-net-worth clients.

▸▸ In-depth consulting and coaching relationships with hedge fund professionals, with an emphasis on the following areas:

   ▸▸ Assisting with the development and implementation of marketing strategies for their funds (as we've defined marketing)

   ▸▸ Working with them to stay focused on their business and personal and professional priorities (*see Appendix A: To Get Wealthy, Stay Centered*); and

   ▸▸ Helping them structure their financial affairs to maximize and protect their personal fortunes (see *Appendix B: Wealth Preservation*).

▸▸ "In the trenches" experience gained during lengthy careers spent working for and with asset managers, institutional investors and the high-net-worth market in a variety of capacities. Please note that we are not, and never have been, third-party marketers or hedge fund sales professionals.

The affluent are our core area of expertise, and by focusing this primer on wealthy individuals and families we are best able to help hedge fund and fund-of-fund firms incorporate the marketing insights we have gleaned after two decades of research, consulting and coaching in this space. We do, however, realize that institutional investors are an important constituent for hedge funds and, as such, have conducted research with them to understand their perspectives more fully. In *Appendix C: Institutional Investors* we include some of the findings from this research initiative.

In the pages that follow, we will share the research we've conducted on affluent hedge fund investors – how they source hedge funds and funds-of-funds, what makes them choose one such fund over another, and why they switch from one fund to another. In effect, it's a look into the minds of affluent hedge fund and fund-of-funds investors. Most importantly, we will outline strategic initiatives that can help you to be significantly more successful in marketing your hedge fund or fund-of-funds.

CONCLUSIONS

Over the past decade, the hedge fund and fund-of-funds industries have grown exponentially when measured by the number of firms in the industry, the number of investors, and the amount of money being managed. What had once been the more or less exclusive realm of a handful of managers and investors has been busted wide open by the outsized returns of the top funds – not to mention the staggering, and seductive, monetary success of the industry's top managers.

With so many more funds to choose from, most affluent investors have naturally become more discerning; they are often no longer necessarily fighting to get into a given hedge fund or fund-of-funds. As a consequence, it makes sense that fund firms become more attentive to marketing as a means of finding and keeping investors, particularly the kind of affluent investor who can also provide quality referrals. By focusing on marketing to such investors, perhaps for the first time, and by fine-tuning that marketing with segmentation data, hedge fund and fund-of-funds firms will be able to stand out in what has become a very crowded field, hold onto clients during downswings, and win the new affluent investors they covet.

SEGMENTING
AFFLUENT INVESTORS

T'S A TRUISM THAT NOT ALL AFFLUENT HEDGE fund or fund-of-funds investors are alike. They have different levels of investment knowledge and sophistication. They have varied experiences investing in funds – and with investing in general. They have preferences, even quirks, unique to their personal realms. At the same time, groups of hedge fund and fund-of-funds investors cluster. That is, there are strong commonalities among certain hedge fund and fund-of-funds investors. In the marketing world, these clusters are referred to as segments.

From a marketing perspective, the ability to leverage these various segments strategically and tactically can prove extremely potent not only when you're raising money but in your efforts to hold onto your investors even when your firm's investment performance is not up to their expectations. Knowing and understanding the client's perspective is critical for any product and service provider, especially for those firms – the vast majority, of course – that want to grow their business and retain their most important clients. By better understanding the various segments, you'll be better able to make informed decisions such as to how to allocate the resources your firm has dedicated to sourcing and "behaviorally locking-in" private wealth. This might translate into not targeting a particular segment or, for another segment, creating a network of high-quality professional referral sources. Segmentation information will also tell you how to best communicate with your wealthy clients on an ongoing basis.

OUR
RESEARCH

In 2007, to learn more about the people who invest in hedge funds and funds-of-funds – and to learn how those fund firms could segment and attract clients – we conducted a survey of 428 wealthy investors with an aggregate investment commitment of US$18 billion to hedge funds or funds-of-funds. On average they invested in 3.3 hedge funds or funds-of-funds with a mean total investment of US$42.1 million and a median investment of US$29.5 million (Exhibit 2.1).

16

EXHIBIT 2.1:
AVERAGE INVESTMENT AMOUNTS
N = 428 AFFLUENT INVESTORS

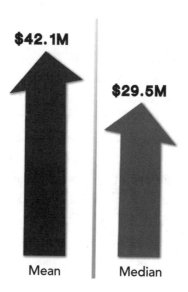

$42.1M

$29.5M

Mean   Median

SEGMENTING
PRIVATE WEALTH

As noted, segmenting target markets is a basic tenet of marketing and it helps companies recognize and exploit the differences and similarities among their customer base. Historically, the hedge fund industry has segmented clients according to their tax status – marketing separately to taxable investors, or the affluent, and to non-taxable investors, or pension funds and not-for-profit organizations – while overlooking other important and influential factors such as the ones we're addressing here.

Broadly speaking, many hedge fund or fund-of-funds investors are similar and, from a statistical standpoint, sizeable groups within the overall universe share characteristics, such as net worth or education level. At the same time, most fund investors also have characteristics that make them distinct from one another. Their levels of investment knowledge and sophistication vary, for example, as do their experiences investing across a range of asset classes and product structures. They also have individual idiosyncrasies and personal nuances that must be taken into account.

17

A deep understanding of various segments can make it easier for you to make informed decisions about, for example, prioritization and resource allocation. Furthermore, the ability to strategically leverage those various segments can prove extremely powerful when raising money.

To that end, using our survey data, we developed an empirically derived segmentation matrix of the affluent hedge fund investing universe that includes two demographic segments, high-net-worth investors and single-family offices, and two behavioral segments, Delegators and Evaluators (Exhibit 2.2).

EXHIBIT 2.2:

THE PRIVATE WEALTH SEGMENTATION MATRIX
N = 428 AFFLUENT INVESTORS

	BEHAVIORAL	
DEMOGRAPHIC	**EVALUATORS**	**DELEGATORS**
High-net-worth investors	**19.8%**	**45.9%**
Single-family offices	**29.0%**	**5.3%**

18

DEMOGRAPHIC
SEGMENTS

High-net-worth investors and single-family offices represent the two demographic segments of today's wealthy hedge fund investors. The largest group of investors in our study was made up of high-net-worth individuals or households that have a portion of their investable assets in hedge funds and funds-of-funds. This group of 281 investors comprised 65.7 percent of the survey sample and had a total of US$7.1 billion invested in hedge funds or funds-of-funds (Exhibit 2.3). On average, they invested in 3.2 hedge funds or funds-of-funds. The average investment by the high-net-worth individual was US$25.4 million with a median investment of US$18.2 million (Exhibit 2.4).

EXHIBIT 2.3:
# DEMOGRAPHIC SEGMENTS
N = 428 AFFLUENT INVESTORS

34.3%
Single-family
offices

65.7%
High-net-worth
investors

EXHIBIT 2.4:
# INVESTMENT AMOUNTS BY
# HIGH-NET-WORTH INVESTORS
N = 281 HIGH-NET-WORTH INVESTORS

19

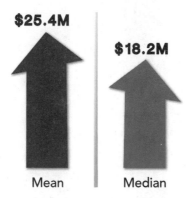

$25.4M

$18.2M

Mean

Median

A single-family office, as its name implies, is the coordinating organization for a single affluent family's wealth and related financial, as well as many non-financial, needs. (For a brief overview of the business model, go to *Appendix D: Hedge Funds, Funds-of-Funds, and the Family Office*). Our survey included 167 single-family offices, which accounted for 34.3 percent of our respondents. The total assets invested in hedge funds or funds-of-funds by the single-family offices in our study was US$10.9 billion. On average, they invested in 3.5 hedge funds or funds-of-funds. The average investment by single-family offices was US$74 million with a median investment of US$51.2 million (Exhibit 2.5).

EXHIBIT 2.5:
INVESTMENT AMOUNTS BY SINGLE-FAMILY OFFICES
N = 167 SINGLE-FAMILY OFFICES

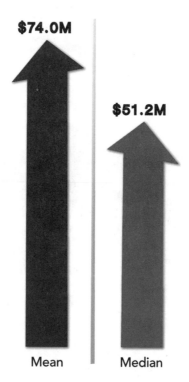

$74.0M — Mean

$51.2M — Median

BEHAVIORAL
SEGMENTS

From a behavioral standpoint, these same hedge fund and fund-of-funds investors fall into one of two categories: Delegators or Evaluators.

As the name indicates, Delegators prefer to rely on the expertise and guidance of professionals and often relinquish most of the decision-making and control of their portfolios to their closest advisors. Evaluators, by contrast, are affluent investors who are actively involved in the oversight and management of their financial affairs, who conduct their own analysis and research, and who generally make the final decisions on important matters. When viewed in total, our hedge fund investors were almost evenly split between Delegators and Evaluators at 51.2 percent and 49.8 percent, respectively (Exhibit 2.6).

EXHIBIT 2.6:
BEHAVIORAL SEGMENTS
N = 428 AFFLUENT INVESTORS

21

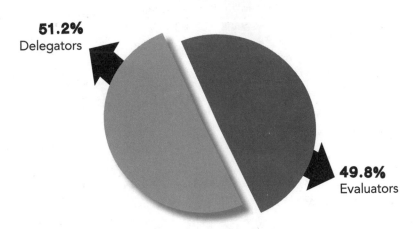

51.2%
Delegators

49.8%
Evaluators

However, the two groups diverged when we asked them how much money they had invested in hedge funds and funds-of-funds. The mean investment by Delegators was US$34.1 million with a median investment of US$23.9 million (Exhibit 2.7), but Evaluators invested far more; the mean investment was US$50.4 million and the median investment was US$35.3 million (Exhibit 2.8).

EXHIBIT 2.7:
INVESTMENT AMOUNTS BY DELEGATORS
N = 219 DELEGATORS

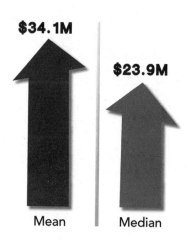

$34.1M

$23.9M

Mean   Median

22

EXHIBIT 2.8:

# INVESTMENT AMOUNTS BY EVALUATORS
N = 209 EVALUATORS

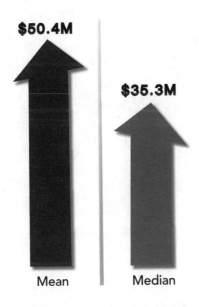

| Mean | Median |

$50.4M — Mean

$35.3M — Median

By way of perspective, it's important to note that the majority of single-family offices (84.4 percent) in our study were Evaluators (Exhibit 2.9), and the majority of high-net-worth investors (69.8 percent) were Delegators (Exhibit 2.10).

23

EXHIBIT 2.9:

BEHAVIORAL BREAKDOWN OF
SINGLE-FAMILY OFFICES
N = 167 SINGLE-FAMILY OFFICES

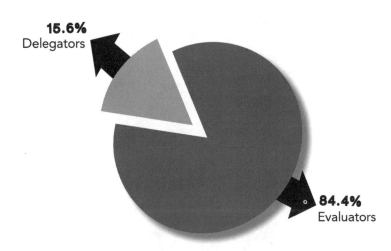

15.6%
Delegators

84.4%
Evaluators

EXHIBIT 2.10:

BEHAVIORAL BREAKDOWN OF
HIGH-NET-WORTH INVESTORS
N = 281 HIGH-NET-WORTH INVESTORS

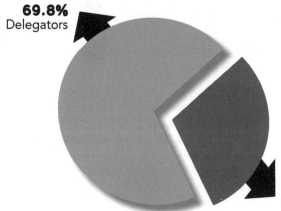

69.8%
Delegators

30.2%
Evaluators

MARKETING IMPLICATIONS
OF SEGMENTATION

The affluent investors in our survey were segmented based on demographics and behavioral criteria so that you can modify your marketing efforts to selectively target these segments in different ways. Even if your firm chooses to pursue all four segments, you are best served by tweaking your approach on a segment-by-segment basis as you market to, and work with, these affluent investors.

Of course, the key to any such marketing efforts is your ability to identify and modify your efforts with respect to the various segments. For example, if you choose to target high-net-worth investors who are Delegators (the largest segment), then you will need to principally source them through their financial advisors. In contrast, if you want to reach the single-family offices that are making all of their own decisions, you're most likely looking at Evaluators. This requires an individualized networking approach and the ability to get into deep technical conversations replete with Greek letters. Further details of the preferences of the four segments and the best ways to reach them will be covered in the chapters that follow.

Lock-ups notwithstanding, most hedge fund firms will find the need to manage the affluent investor experience at one time or another, and each segment requires a somewhat different approach in this regard.

25

CONCLUSIONS

"One size doesn't fit all." While most professionals would agree, we have found that most hedge fund and fund-of-funds firms approach their clients as being taxable (i.e., affluent) or non-taxable (i.e., institutions such as pension funds and eleemosynary organizations), assuming they make any distinctions at all, which doesn't allow for sufficient customization based on how and why they invest.

However, as we'll see throughout the rest of this book, consistently successful marketing is predicated on differential actions based on the buying and behavioral patterns of definable affluent investor segments.

When it comes to affluent hedge fund and fund-of-funds investors, we were able to develop the private wealth segmentation matrix. Consequently, we have two demographic segments – single-family offices and high-net-worth investors. We also have two behavioral segments – Delegators and Evaluators. Your ability to raise money from the wealthy, not to mention your ability to hold onto that money dramatically increases if you employ marketing methodologies based on this more precise affluent segmentation.

SOURCING
AFFLUENT
INVESTORS

AS WE HAVE ALREADY NOTED, FIRMS THAT offer hedge funds and funds-of-funds have to work a lot harder to land affluent clients – the right affluent clients – these days than was previously the case when wealthy investors were jostling to get into one of the small number of funds before they were closed to new business. The information in this chapter is designed to help such firms reformulate their marketing initiatives to attract those affluent investors in the face of greater competition and more investor options.

To see what works from the client standpoint, we evaluated the importance of various methods the affluent used to find and learn about hedge fund and fund-of-funds investments (Exhibit 3.1). The clear-cut winner was a financial advisor, cited by 63.8 percent of the respondents. Personal networking and research was the runner-up, cited by 48.8 percent of investors.

The other methods were less pervasive and therefore likely to be less successful in yielding satisfactory results. However, it's important to recognize that these other methods can be "additive." Hearing about a fund from one's financial advisor, for instance, and then hearing about it from one's accountant will increase the likelihood that the affluent investor will take a serious look at the hedge fund in question. Similarly, if a single-family office through its networking efforts hears of a particular fund-of-funds and that fund-of-funds is highlighted at a conference, the decision to consider that fund is reinforced.

EXHIBIT 3.1:

"VERY" OR "EXTREMELY" IMPORTANT SOURCES FOR SELECTING HEDGE FUNDS AND FUNDS-OF-FUNDS
N = 428 AFFLUENT INVESTORS

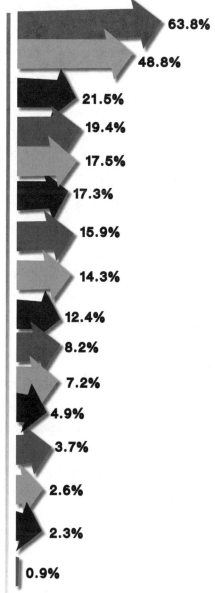

Source	Percentage
A financial advisor	63.8%
Their own networking or research activities	48.8%
An investment management consultant	21.5%
An accountant	19.4%
Seminars and conferences	17.5%
Business associates	17.3%
Third-party marketers	15.9%
Hedge fund data-bases	14.3%
A capital introductions professional	12.4%
An attorney	8.2%
Other types of professionals	7.2%
The Internet	4.9%
Stories about the hedge fund or fund-of-funds in the media	3.7%
Friends and/or family members	2.6%
Other hedge fund or fund-of-funds firms	2.3%
Cold calls from the hedge fund or fund-of-funds firms	0.9%

30

It's important to note, however, that some of the approaches that are effective with respect to institutional investors are much less so when dealing with affluent investors. For instance, capital introductions professionals tend to introduce hedge funds to institutions and while some single-family offices can be considered institutions, by and large, these professionals have very limited access to that world.

Armed with this knowledge, in general, hedge fund and fund-of-funds firms can retool their marketing efforts to be more inclusive of advisors, position themselves in the path of wealthy investors that conduct their own research, and be more mindful of existing affluent clients who can provide referrals. But while any or all of these changes would be a step in the right direction, they would not be sufficient in and of themselves. To have a complete profile of their target markets and to build a foundation for tailored business development initiatives, hedge fund and fund-of-funds firms must also know more about the demographics and behavioral preferences of their targeted wealthy clients.

31

DEMOGRAPHIC
CONSIDERATIONS

Demographic factors play a significant role in the way that affluent investors find hedge funds and funds-of-funds. The following table shows the methods for sourcing hedge funds with a break-down between high-net-worth investors and single-family offices (Exhibit 3.2). The results show that advisors were most important to individuals, whereas single-family offices, which are more likely to be staffed with financial professionals, were understandably more inclined to rely on their own expertise when finding and evaluating new investment products. Family offices will, however, also turn to consultants to help them assess a range of financial products against their stated objectives.

EXHIBIT 3.2:

SOURCING FUNDS BY DEMOGRAPHIC SEGMENTS
N = 428 AFFLUENT INVESTORS

SOURCE	HNWs	SFOs
A financial advisor	84.0%	25.2%
Their own networking or research activities	30.2%	84.4%
An investment management consultant	5.7%	51.7%
An accountant	21.4%	15.6%
Seminars and conferences	11.0%	29.9%
Business associates	14.6%	22.4%
Third-party marketers	13.2%	21.1%
Hedge fund data-bases	7.8%	26.5%
A capital introductions professional	4.3%	27.9%
An attorney	4.6%	15.0%
Other types of professionals	3.9%	13.6%
The Internet	4.3%	6.1%
Stories about the hedge fund or fund-of-funds in the media	4.3%	2.7%
Friends and/or family members	1.1%	5.4%
Other hedge fund or fund-of-funds firms	1.1%	4.8%
Cold calls from the hedge fund or fund-of-funds firms	0.0%	2.7%

BEHAVIORAL
CONSIDERATIONS

When the data was further broken down by behavioral segment, we found that all of the Evaluators – without exception – conducted their own networking and research to source new products, and complemented that initiative with other sources of information such as advisors, seminars, and databases (Exhibit 3.3). Most Delegators, by contrast, turned to advice practitioners for research recommendations. In fact, nearly 88 percent of Delegators said they used a financial advisor to source new hedge funds. Interestingly, the methods cited second (18.3 percent) and fourth (12.8 percent) by Delegators were other types of advisors – accountants and investment management consultants – reinforcing the importance of outside experts to this behavioral segment.

EXHIBIT 3.3:
SOURCING FUNDS BY BEHAVIORAL SEGMENTS
N = 428 AFFLUENT INVESTORS

33

SOURCE	DELEGATORS	EVALUATORS
A financial advisor	87.7%	38.8%
Their own networking or research activities	0.0%	100.0%
An investment management consultant	12.8%	30.6%
An accountant	18.3%	20.6%
Seminars and conferences	0.5%	35.4%
Business associates	6.8%	28.2%
Third-party marketers	14.2%	17.7%
Hedge fund data-bases	0.0%	29.2%
A capital introductions professional	3.2%	22.0%

SOURCE	DELEGATORS	EVALUATORS
An attorney	1.8%	14.8%
Other types of professionals	1.4%	13.4%
The Internet	0.0%	10.0%
Stories about the hedge fund or fund-of-funds in the media	0.9%	6.7%
Friends and/or family members	1.8%	3.3%
Other hedge fund or fund-of-funds firms	0.0%	4.8%
Cold calls from the hedge fund or fund-of-funds firms	0.0%	1.9%

34

INTERMEDIARIES AS A
PRIMARY CONDUIT TO
HIGH-NET-WORTH INVESTORS

As a segment, 84 percent of high-net-worth investors turned to financial advisors for direction when seeking hedge funds and funds-of-funds. As a result, fund firms with an interest in further accessing the universe of high-net-worth investors would be well advised to build relationships with trusted advisors to the wealthy.

Many hedge funds and funds-of-funds have sales and service efforts focused on various types of advisors, including brokers, registered investment advisors, insurance agents, financial planners, accountants, and attorneys. Unfortunately, according to 88.7 percent of financial advisors themselves, these efforts are largely ineffective (Exhibit 3.4). To a large degree this is due to inexperienced third-party marketers, sales professionals and wholesalers, one-size-fits-all presentations, and aggressive sales tactics and product positioning that leave little room for productive dialogue or interaction (Exhibit 3.5).

EXHIBIT 3.4:

INEFFECTIVE SALES EFFORTS
TARGETING FINANCIAL ADVISORS
N = 302 FINANCIAL ADVISORS

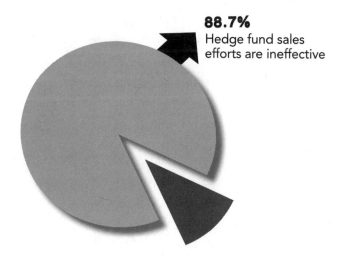

88.7%
Hedge fund sales
efforts are ineffective

EXHIBIT 3.5:

REASONS FOR FAILURE
N = 302 FINANCIAL ADVISORS

The funds do not
understand their
businesses
95.7%

The "sales
professionals"
were lacking
73.8%

The presentation
was generic and
uninformative
65.9%

The approach
was too "pushy"
48.7%

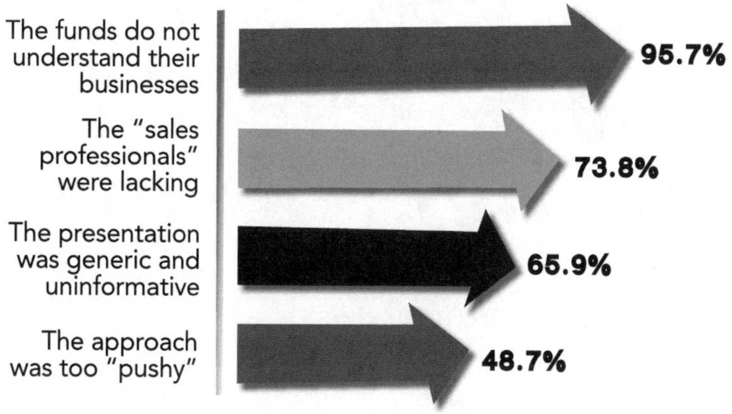

Our extensive research with advisors coupled with decades of experience coaching the very best practitioners shows that a more targeted and customized approach based on advance preparation – that is, a detailed understanding of their business models and clientele – will yield better results for the firms that want to work with them. Furthermore, systematizing this process will allow it to be refined and mastered by the hedge fund and fund-of-funds firms that employ it. Consequently, we believe that fund firms should be very selective when establishing strategic partnerships with advisors, rather than simply agreeing to distribute funds broadly through any type of practitioner (Exhibit 3.6). When developing a professional relationship, it is important that both parties have similar levels of commitment to the partnership and figure centrally into one another's business plans. That is the definition of a strategic partnership as opposed to a strategic alliance.

EXHIBIT 3.6:
COMPARING THE STRATEGIC ALLIANCE
TO THE STRATEGIC PARTNERSHIP

STRATEGIC ALLIANCE	STRATEGIC PARTNERSHIP
Infrequently providing hedge funds to clients	Actively looking for clients for whom the fund is a good fit
Fund is one of a number of possible comparable alternative investments made available to clients	Fund is the preferred offering of its type on the advisor's platform
Have numerous, low-productivity distribution relationships	Work selectively and productively with a few providers

RETHINKING
THE RELATIONSHIP

Before embarking on an effort to build strategic partnerships, fund firms need to modify both their thinking and approach to working with financial advisors. Specifically, they need to realize that:

▶▶ The hedge fund or fund-of-funds firms should select the financial advisors best suited for a partnership, rather than waiting for financial advisors to select them.

▶▶ The financial advisor must be treated like a client, in much the same way a high-net-worth investor or a single-family office is a client.

▶▶ A partnership is not solely about new business referrals but should be recognized as a joint-working relationship.

▶▶ Once the correct financial advisors have been identified, it should be understood that a comparatively small number will yield a very high volume and quality of business.

37

Over the long term, the strategic partnership will require more than investment results from the hedge fund or fund-of-funds to sustain itself and fund providers will have to deliver added value to the relationship.

THE
PROFILING
PROCESS

A key part of building strategic relationships is a comprehensive profiling process. You must complete this effort with each advisor you have identified as a plausible strategic partner, gathering data via in-depth interviews and conducting an informed assessment of the advisor's ability to be an effective partner to your firm. The types of information and topics that must be addressed during the profiling process include:

» The size of the advisor's practice as measured in assets under management and number of affluent clients, including the number of accredited investors.

» Demographics on the advisor such as age, experience, education, licensing, areas of expertise, marital status, key relationships, and income.

» The advisor's stated and unstated goals and objectives for his or her practice.

» Their professional perspective and biases on a range of financial services and products.

» The advisor's existing product offerings and provider relationships.

» The strengths and weaknesses of their practice management and marketing approaches.

» Their source of compensation and its relationship to their decision-making and lifestyle.

» The profile and source of their key investors.

» An overview of their existing sub-advisory relationships, including hedge fund and fund-of-funds firms.

» Their perspective on, and willingness to enter, strategic partnerships with other hedge fund and fund-of-funds firms.

Over time, this process becomes a potent way for fund firms to connect with the financial advisors who can deliver desirable affluent investors and also builds long-term relationships with professionals and wealthy investors that can be sustained regardless of investment performance. It's important to note that this process has proven extremely effective for reaching high-net-worth investors, but is not as suitable for accessing the single-family offices due to their more limited involvement with, and reliance on, these types of financial advisors.

TAPPING INTO
THE NETWORKS OF
SINGLE-FAMILY OFFICES

With a strong focus on their own networking and research activities in finding hedge funds and funds-of-funds, a different approach is usually called for when it comes to reaching single-family offices. Many single-family offices make concerted efforts to build connections with each other. The motivations for this vary but they include:

▸▸ Co-investing,

▸▸ Obtaining services at lower rates, and

▸▸ Gathering industry intelligence.

In our research with single-family offices, we have found that the mean number of other such offices they had strong relationships with was 5.9 and the median number was 4.1 (Exhibit 3.7). A strong relationship is defined as one where the single-family office will discuss investments, including hedge funds and funds-of-funds, with other offices at least six times a year.

39

EXHIBIT 3.7:

THE NUMBER OF STRONG RELATIONSHIPS WITH OTHER SINGLE-FAMILY OFFICES
N = 147 SINGLE-FAMILY OFFICES

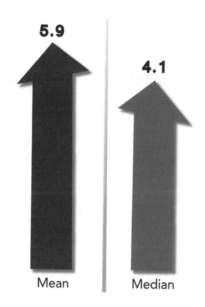

5.9

4.1

Mean   Median

With respect to these strong relationships, alternative investments – especially hedge funds and funds-of-funds – were regularly recommended, with those recommendations being accepted an impressive 66.9 percent of the time (Exhibit 3.8).

EXHIBIT 3.8:
OTHER SINGLE-FAMILY OFFICES ACCEPTING ALTERNATIVE INVESTMENT RECOMMENDATIONS
N = 147 SINGLE-FAMILY OFFICES

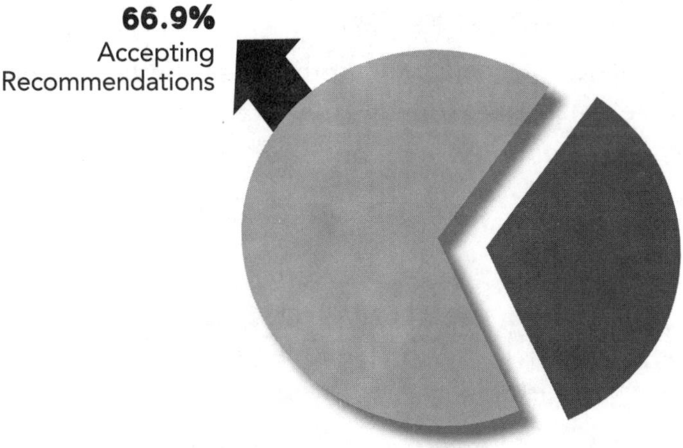

Of course, for this information to be of any value, it is essential to determine the network of similar single-family offices each single-family office has a strong relationship with. Part of our ongoing work with family offices includes the construction and use of sociograms to help us understand the connections and relational valences between offices based on the core characteristics of each, including:

- Assets under management,
- Previous experiences with hedge funds and funds-of-funds,
- The array of services and products provided to family members,
- Internal investment management capabilities,
- Investment out-sourcing experience,

▸▸ Their motivation to associate with other family offices,

▸▸ The motivation of the wealthy family to have established a single-family office, and

▸▸ The ability to get a meeting with the single-family office.

The output from the statistical model is used to assess the quality of the connection between the single-family offices. With this information in hand, we can then help hedge funds and other asset managers identify the strongest candidates for potential new business and prioritize them accordingly for introductions.

A NOTE ON
MULTI-FAMILY OFFICES

When we conducted our broad-based survey of the family office universe, we defined multi-family offices as family offices where there was an anchor family with a stake of at least 30 percent in the operation. There are many multi-family offices that hedge fund and fund-of-funds firms can focus on. Many multi-family offices are a hybrid between a financial advisor and a single-family office – with the emphasis on the financial advisor. Still, we've found that the strategy of evaluating intermediaries (discussed above) is the optimal way to go. By considering the multi-family office as an intermediary (with significant decision-making authority), you will be able to apprise its individual business model and identify and quantify opportunities for your fund.

Moreover, there are multi-family offices we refer to as the "Fringe," that not only control huge sums of money but also have unique cultural characteristics (see *Appendix E: Scenes from the Fringe*) that can enhance the relationship between members, families and other fringe organizations.

CONCLUSIONS

When looking for new affluent clients, our research has shown that the most direct route is by way of financial advisors. This is not to suggest that there is no value in other potential points of entry, a seminar or the Internet, for example, but that the latter are of greater value when they are added to the weight of an advisor's recommendation.

However, for fund firms to create productive relationships with advisors – those that lead to long-standing and profitable clients – the relationships must progress from a simple working alliance to a powerful strategic partnership. And to get there, the fund firm must invest the extra time and manpower to find and vet the advisors whom it will partner with, upfront due diligence that can lead to high quality partnerships.

Single-family offices are far less likely to be reliant on financial advisors – they have their own "advisors" in house. But they do network with one another and, if a fund firm can get the attention and business of one single-family office, they can often obtain referrals to other single-family offices.

43

SELECTING
HEDGE FUNDS AND
FUNDS-OF-FUNDS

FOR HEDGE FUNDS AND FUNDS-OF-FUNDS FIRMS, performance is paramount; indeed, it used to be the only thing that mattered because investors vied for the right to get into the best funds before they were closed to new money. But with that success came heightened competition and a pitched battle for high-end investors who suddenly had a range of funds to choose from. So, as part of our research, we empirically evaluated what went into the decision-making of affluent investors: when it came to hedge funds and funds-of-funds, which ones did they choose and why?

Given the high cost of entry and the number of very specific investment strategies, it's not surprising that nearly all of the wealthy investors we surveyed invested in their hedge funds or funds-of-funds as part of a broader investment planning initiative (Exhibit 4.1). That is, by and large, the decision to invest was part of an overall asset allocation process. Often, the greatest benefit a hedge fund or fund-of-funds can provide its owner is its non-correlated performance relative to other parts of a portfolio – an opportunity missed were it purchased at random and without consideration for other investments. Far fewer investors cited other types of processes as the impetus behind their ownership of a hedge fund or fund-of-funds: only 35 percent referred to a more expansive financial planning process and less than 25 percent of the investors surveyed cited more targeted efforts such as asset protection or charitable giving.

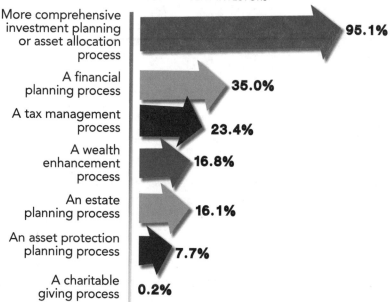

EXHIBIT 4.1:
PROCESS USED
N = 428 AFFLUENT INVESTORS

Process	Percentage
More comprehensive investment planning or asset allocation process	95.1%
A financial planning process	35.0%
A tax management process	23.4%
A wealth enhancement process	16.8%
An estate planning process	16.1%
An asset protection planning process	7.7%
A charitable giving process	0.2%

48

PART OF AN
INVESTMENT MANAGEMENT
APPROACH

The breadth and depth of a single-family office's financial responsibilities and input came to light when we looked at the processes used by demographic segment – high-net worth investors as opposed to single-family offices. Again, 95 percent of wealthy individuals cited an overall investment or asset allocation strategy as their path to a hedge fund or fund-of-funds, and almost half also mentioned a financial planning effort (Exhibit 4.2). But while a similar percentage of single-family offices referred to their overarching investment planning as playing an influential role, about half also cited two processes that were of little consequence to high-net-worth investors: their efforts to mitigate taxes and to enhance wealth. Furthermore, about one-quarter of single-family offices also used hedge funds or funds-of-funds as part of their estate planning and asset protection processes.

EXHIBIT 4.2:

PROCESS USED BY DEMOGRAPHIC SEGMENTS
N = 428 AFFLUENT INVESTORS

EXTENSIVE	HNWs	SFOs
A more comprehensive investment planning or asset allocation process	95.0%	95.2%
A financial planning process	48.4%	9.5%
A tax management process	9.6%	49.7%
A wealth enhancement process	0.0%	49.0%
An estate planning process	10.3%	27.2%
An asset protection planning process	0.0%	22.4%
A charitable giving process	0.4%	0.0%

49

DELEGATORS AND
EVALUATORS

Those results remained fairly constant when viewed by behavioral segments. Almost all Delegators cited an investment or asset allocation plan as the rationale behind their investing in a hedge fund or fund-of-funds (Exhibit 4.3). And, furthermore, about half of the Delegators mentioned a financial plan. The results for Evaluators, however, were similar to the responses from the single-family office segment, albeit with slightly fewer naming tax management and wealth enhancement processes as relevant to their purchase of a hedge fund.

EXHIBIT 4.3

PROCESS USED BY BEHAVIORAL SEGMENTS

N = 428 AFFLUENT INVESTORS

EXTENSIVE	DELEGATORS	EVALUATORS
A more comprehensive investment planning or asset allocation process	97.7%	92.3%
A financial planning process	48.9%	20.6%
A tax management process	15.5%	31.6%
A wealth enhancement process	4.1%	30.1%
An estate planning process	13.7%	18.7%
An asset protection planning process	2.3%	13.4%
A charitable giving process	0.0%	0.5%

Returning to the financial advisors we surveyed, we found that all of them employ some sort of investment planning or asset allocation approach when incorporating hedge funds or funds-of-funds into the portfolios of their affluent clients. For those we surveyed, the percentage range of a wealthy client's investment portfolio allocated to hedge funds or funds-of-funds ran from 12 percent on the low side to 63 percent on the high side. The mean percentage was 42.3 percent with a median of 24.5 percent (Exhibit 4.4).

EXHIBIT 4.4:

CLIENT PORTFOLIO ALLOCATIONS TO HEDGE FUNDS
N = 302 FINANCIAL ADVISORS

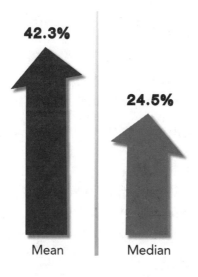

42.3% — Mean

24.5% — Median

THE NEED FOR A
CONSULTATIVE
APPROACH

51

From a marketing standpoint, this signals the value of promoting hedge funds and funds-of-funds consultatively and suggests that focusing on their roles and advantages in an affluent client's total portfolio will often prove worthwhile. This entails going beyond just pitching the fund to understanding how the fund will function as part of, and relative to the rest of, the affluent client's portfolio.

Adopting a consultative perspective requires focusing on the reasons the affluent client is investing and – by and large – it's more then simply "making money." Generally, there are specific reasons for wanting to make more money or preserve wealth.

What you need to do is think in terms of how your hedge fund or fund-of-funds fits into the holistic investment and, maybe holistic, needs and wants of the affluent. Operationally, this is more about evaluating then explaining. When it comes to the wealthy, the most successful professional advisors are laser-focused on knowing the "hot buttons" of their clients and using them as a framework for presenting their recommendations. This means that simply outlining the attributes of your fund – in effect, explaining the fund – proves to be generally not all that productive.

The exception being situations where your fund has been invited to compete for a specific, well-defined piece of business. For the most part, this is only going to happen when you're dealing with Delegators. In effect, the financial advisor is bringing you to a Delegator to make your presentation and answer questions. However, it's critical to realize that the financial advisors have a considerable amount of influence in the process.

The result of being consultative is that you can better understand the affluent investor's motivations, needs, and wants when it comes to his or her making investment decisions. In many cases, this means you will have to work through intermediaries such as financial advisors and even, sometimes, an executive of a single-family office. Nevertheless, such an approach is valid for it will enable you to put into context your hedge fund or fund-of-funds in a way that makes them much more appealing and compelling.

SELECTION
CRITERIA

Simply knowing that a broad-based planning process plays an important role in an affluent investor's purchase of a hedge fund or fund-of-fund is rarely in and of itself enough to understand why they own a specific fund. To get a better read on the individual criteria that high-net-worth investors and single-family offices rely on when evaluating and selecting a fund, we asked them to evaluate 26 factors and the importance that each played in their ultimate investment decision.

We found that the number one piece of information used by affluent investors when evaluating a hedge fund or fund-of-funds was the strategy used by the investment team, registering with 84.3 percent of our respondents (Exhibit 4.6). As we stated, the hedge fund business is about investment performance, and that performance is driven by the manager's investment approach or strategy. What's important to note is that while the investment strategy or approach is rated highly by more of the affluent than any other factor, your ability to communicate the strategy or approach was only deemed "very" or "extremely" important by slightly less than one-half the affluent investors we surveyed. As we'll see, this is where segmentation provides the explanation.

More than three-quarters of the hedge fund investors surveyed also noted the importance of a professional's recommendation, the hedge fund manager's investment philosophy, how well the fund fit into their existing portfolio of investments, and the quality of the teams to whom they entrusted their money. That's not to say that other factors don't play an influential role in the selection process, they do, and the relevance of each should not be underestimated; even if they are not the "make-or-break" factors, they still matter. Consequently, when proposing hedge funds or funds-of-funds to affluent investors, these other factors should also – selectively – be made part of the story (see below).

At the far end of the spectrum, however, there are a number of factors that were clearly of little or no importance to hedge fund and fund-of-funds investors. For instance, the business structure of the hedge fund firm was less pertinent to investors (22.2 percent). That distinction was of little importance because the majority of hedge fund and fund-of-funds investors know that many of the most competitive products come from boutique operations, and that simultaneously the hedge fund industry is experiencing some consolidation as larger institutions acquire fund firms to expand their investment capabilities and make themselves more attractive to affluent investors. In short, serious affluent investors acknowledge that the industry is in flux, but it doesn't matter to them.

Affluent investors were also not likely to be swayed by the recommendations of business associates (7.7 percent) or family members and friends (2.3 percent) – most of whom do not possess the expertise to accurately assess the appropriateness of a specific investment for another individual. Once you get past "friends and family fundraising," these relationships are usually not very useful in garnering additional assets.

Lastly, a product's registration status with the SEC was almost at the bottom of the list in terms of its significance when investors were evaluating a fund (7.0 percent). That's not surprising as most hedge funds and funds-of-funds are private placements that don't require registration, and investors at this level of wealth and sophistication have likely already had experience with similar structures.

EXHIBIT 4.6:

"VERY" OR "EXTREMELY" IMPORTANT SELECTION CRITERIA

N = 428 AFFLUENT INVESTORS

CRITERION	PERCENTAGE
The investment approach or strategy	84.3%
The recommendation of a professional advisor	80.6%
The investment philosophy of the managers	77.8%
The appropriateness or fit of the hedge fund or fund-of-funds into your investment portfolio	76.2%
The quality of the people running the hedge fund or fund-of-funds	75.2%
The track record of the managers	72.2%
The manager has a significant personal stake in the hedge fund or fund-of-funds	57.0%
Your analysis and assessment of the hedge fund or fund-of-funds	49.8%
The background of the managers	49.5%
Their explanation of their approach or strategy	46.7%
The way the hedge fund or fund-of-funds manages risk	35.0%
The fact that the hedge fund or fund-of-funds is not correlated with your other investments	32.5%
The fee structure of the hedge fund or fund-of-funds	27.8%
Their use of leverage	25.7%
The way the hedge fund or fund-of-funds firm is structured	22.2%
The hedge fund or fund-of-funds firm's attentiveness to tax issues	19.4%
The length of the lock-up period	18.0%
The vendors the hedge fund or fund-of-funds firm is using	16.6%

CRITERION	PERCENTAGE
The amount of assets the hedge fund or fund-of-funds firm is managing	11.4%
The age of the hedge fund or fund-of-funds	10.0%
Transparency	9.6%
The recommendation of a business associate	7.7%
Registered with the Securities and Exchange Commission	7.0%
The hedge fund or fund-of-funds firm is a boutique operation	2.8%
The hedge fund or fund-of-funds firm is part of a larger financial services organization	2.6%
The recommendation of a friend or family member	2.3%

56

SELECTION CRITERIA BY
DEMOGRAPHIC SEGMENT

When viewing the importance of selection criteria by demographic and behavioral segments, some profound differences arose that should be considered closely by hedge funds and funds-of-funds firms as they develop their marketing strategies. Both high-net-worth individuals and single-family offices cited the same top five items as meaningful in their selection process, along with the performance record of the managers (Exhibit 4.7). After that, there were a number of factors that carried less weight for the high-net-worth but weighed heavily for the single-family offices due to their institutional-quality investment processes. Those items included the office's own analysis and assessment of a product (cited by 85.0 percent of the single-family offices), how well the investment team articulated its strategy (75.5 percent), how much of a personal stake management had in its own product (70.7 percent), and the credentials of the management team (68.7 percent). Of less importance, but still cited by more than half of the single-family offices, were a fund's risk management process (55.8 percent), its tax-advantaged status (54.4 percent), and its correlation to other specific investments (52.4 percent).

EXHIBIT 4.7:
SELECTION CRITERIA BY DEMOGRAPHIC SEGMENTS
N = 428 AFFLUENT INVESTORS

CRITERION	HNWs	SFOs
The investment approach or strategy	82.6%	87.8%
The recommendation of a professional advisor	88.3%	66.0%
The investment philosophy of the managers	72.6%	87.8%
The appropriateness or fit of the hedge fund or fund-of-funds into your investment portfolio	72.2%	83.7%
The quality of the people running the hedge fund or fund-of-funds	71.9%	81.6%
The track record of the managers	65.1%	85.7%
The manager has a significant personal stake in the hedge fund or fund-of-funds	49.8%	70.7%
Your analysis and assessment of the hedge fund or fund-of-funds	31.3%	85.0%
The background of the managers	39.5%	68.7%
Their explanation of their approach or strategy	31.7%	75.5%
The way the hedge fund or fund-of-funds manages risk	24.2%	55.8%
The fact that the hedge fund or fund-of-funds is not correlated with your other investments	22.1%	52.4%
The fee structure of the hedge fund or fund-of-funds	21.4%	40.1%
Their use of leverage	21.7%	33.3%

57

CRITERION	HNWs	SFOs
The way the hedge fund or fund-of-funds firm is structured	15.3%	35.4%
The hedge fund or fund-of-funds firm's attentiveness to tax issues	1.1%	54.4%
The length of the lock-up period	20.3%	13.6%
The vendors the hedge fund or fund-of-funds firm is using	7.8%	33.3%
The amount of assets the hedge fund or fund-of-funds firm is managing	11.7%	10.9%
The age of the hedge fund or fund-of-funds	7.5%	15.0%
Transparency	5.7%	17.0%
The recommendation of a business associate	8.9%	5.4%
Registered with the Securities and Exchange Commission	6.8%	7.5%
The hedge fund or fund-of-funds firm is a boutique operation	2.5%	3.4%
The hedge fund or fund-of-funds firm is part of a larger financial services organization	2.1%	3.4%
The recommendation of a friend or family member	1.4%	4.1%

58

SELECTION CRITERIA BY
BEHAVIORAL SEGMENT

Viewing the importance of fund selection criteria by behavioral segment may provide the clearest picture of how affluent investors make decisions. As it happened, every Delegator surveyed said that an advisor's recommendation had the greatest impact on his or her decision to buy a specific fund (compared to only 60.3 percent of Evaluators), and every Evaluator surveyed relied most heavily on his or her own expertise when analyzing and assessing potential products (compared to just 1.8 percent of Delegators) (Exhibit 4.8).

EXHIBIT 4.8:

# SELECTION CRITERIA BY BEHAVIORAL SEGMENTS
N = 428 AFFLUENT INVESTORS

CRITERION	DELEGATORS	EVALUATORS
The investment approach or strategy	77.2%	91.9%
The recommendation of a professional advisor	100.0%	60.3%
The investment philosophy of the managers	70.3%	85.6%
The appropriateness or fit of the hedge fund or fund-of-funds into your investment portfolio	78.1%	74.2%
The quality of the people running the hedge fund or fund-of-funds	75.3%	75.1%
The track record of the managers	57.1%	88.0%
The manager has a significant personal stake in the hedge fund or fund-of-funds	44.3%	70.3%
Your analysis and assessment of the hedge fund or fund-of-funds	1.8%	100.0%
The background of the managers	29.7%	70.3%
Their explanation of their approach or strategy	6.4%	89.0%
The way the hedge fund or fund-of-funds manages risk	12.3%	58.9%
The fact that the hedge fund or fund-of-funds is not correlated with your other investments	12.3%	53.6%
The fee structure of the hedge fund or fund-of-funds	13.7%	42.6%
Their use of leverage	5.9%	46.4%
The way the hedge fund or fund-of-funds firm is structured	5.5%	39.7%

CRITERION	DELEGATORS	EVALUATORS
The hedge fund or fund-of-funds firm's attentiveness to tax issues	6.4%	33.0%
The length of the lock-up period	8.7%	27.8%
The vendors the hedge fund or fund-of-funds firm is using	0.0%	34.0%
The amount of assets the hedge fund or fund-of-funds firm is managing	4.6%	18.7%
The age of the hedge fund or fund-of-funds	2.7%	17.7%
Transparency	1.8%	17.7%
The recommendation of a business associate	7.3%	8.1%
Registered with the Securities and Exchange Commission	1.8%	12.4%
The hedge fund or fund-of-funds firm is a boutique operation	3.7%	1.9%
The hedge fund or fund-of-funds firm is part of a larger financial services organization	3.2%	1.9%
The recommendation of a friend or family member	2.7%	1.9%

THE NEED TO
DEMONSTRATE CONTINUITY

Using factor analysis, we discovered an underlying concern of affluent hedge fund and fund-of-funds investors. More than ever these investors are concerned about the continuity of the fund investment process and operations if there is a change in the investment staff. This proves to be even more important when the hedge fund has less than US$750 million under management.

In total, 48.3 percent of affluent investors and single-family offices were concerned about continuity, but it was far more of a factor for single-family offices at 68.7 percent than for high-net-worth investors at 32.7 percent (Exhibit 4.9). Meanwhile, an even greater number of financial advisors, 75.8 percent, were concerned about investment talent continuity, which is obviously an important factor given the reliance of most investors on advisors for guidance (Exhibit 4.10).

EXHIBIT 4.9:
AFFLUENT INVESTORS CONCERNED WITH FUND CONTINUITY
N = 428 AFFLUENT INVESTORS

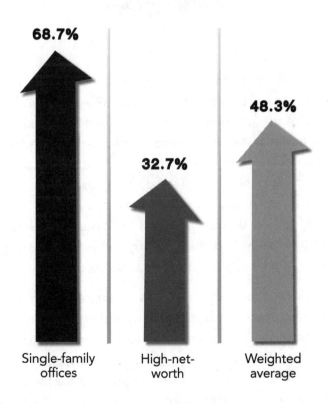

68.7%	32.7%	48.3%
Single-family offices	High-net-worth	Weighted average

61

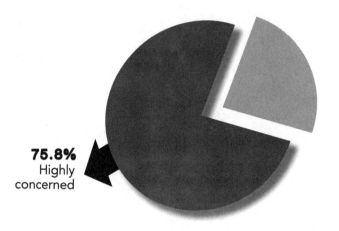

EXHIBIT 4.10:
FINANCIAL ADVISORS CONCERNED
WITH FUND CONTINUITY
N = 302 FINANCIAL ADVISORS

75.8%
Highly
concerned

62

This is an issue that has marketing implications but – in certain circumstances – can significantly affect the personal financial situations of the partners in the management companies. We regularly find that the partnership agreements fail to effectively, or even adequately, address the transfer of shares of the management company in the event of the death or disability of a partner. While there are usually some arrangements in place, they are, very often, not well thought through from a business perspective. We also frequently find that the buy/sell agreements – when they exist – are poorly constructed and improperly funded.

As the hedge fund industry continues to mature, affluent investors are becoming more sensitive to safeguarding their monies and avoiding problems if something were to happen to the investment talent of a fund. From a marketing perspective, the ability to explain precisely what would happen if a key member of the management company left the firm, were to die, or become disabled is becoming a bigger and more important issue.

STORYWORK

Once the selection criteria used by affluent investors in selecting hedge funds and funds-of-funds has been identified, it can be used to develop actionable presentations that will resonate with high-net-worth investors (and their advisors) as well as single-family offices. This process is referred to as "Storywork."

Storywork is the art of crafting the proper marketing message for the prospective affluent investor given his or her unique circumstances or situation.

The more personalized the Storywork, the higher perception of value on the part of the affluent investor. Successful Storywork is predicated on customizing messages to each of the demographic or behavioral segments.

Our research proves useful in setting the stage and providing a platform from which you can construct your fund's, or your firm's, unique story.

63

The story needs to have striking imagery and a message potent with promise. Key to the promise is fund performance. That is, the implicit belief that the fund will deliver.

Considering affluent investors in the aggregate, Storywork should focus on the investment approach or strategy, the investment philosophy of the managers, and the appropriateness of the fund in the client's investment portfolio. Investment performance *per se* should not necessarily be the exclusive focus. Moreover, by making Storywork about these factors, you are setting the stage to manage the affluent investor's expectations. This proves critical when investment performance is lacking (see *Chapter 7: Creating Highly Satisfied Affluent Investors*).

Part of crafting an effective story is addressing the breath and depth of the hedge fund or fund-of-funds. For instance, relatively few managers address their side pocket investments. One hedge fund firm found that incorporating its investment in movies into its presentation proved to be very powerful when raising money. Another one found intense interest from investors in the music catalogues it was acquiring. A third hedge fund firm found that discussing its investments in financing vehicles incorporating special purpose entities was an effective part of gathering assets. While all of these investments represented less than 10 percent of the respective fund portfolios, they turned out to be good starting points for conversations. However, each story connected the side pocket investments to the principal investment strategy of the fund and it was that interconnectedness that helped seal the deal.

In developing the story for your fund, there are three core elements you need to include. They are:

➤➤ The investment rationale of your hedge fund or fund-of-funds. In effect, this is about your investment strategy and approach. However, it's not enough to just describe it; you must validate it. This is where your firm will also talk about its track record or, at least, its back-tested results.

➤➤ The way you will execute and deliver results. Here you need to address the investment talent that will produce the investment performance. Even in the case of a purely quantitative approach, the computer programs that will deliver investment returns need to be described.

➤➤ The appropriate affluent client. Being an accredited investor is woefully insufficient as your firm wouldn't even consider a person who wasn't. What we're considering here ties into the wealthy investor's overall portfolio. What is the affluent investor looking for – or in need of – and how does your hedge fund or fund-of-funds work for them? In effect, for whom is your fund most appropriate?

All the various selection criteria are interwoven within these three elements. Additionally, by being consultative, you're able to individualize the story. When you're able to develop and deliver the story as described, the result is a highly customized, interactive presentation that translates into far greater sales.

CONCLUSIONS

Just as distinct types of hedge fund and fund-of-funds investors source their products in different ways, distinct affluent investor segments rely on their own set of evaluation criteria when it comes to deciding which fund to invest, or not invest, in. Based on these preferences, you can customize marketing efforts that more precisely target, for example, high-net-worth individuals as opposed to single-family offices, or Evaluators as opposed to Delegators.

To effectively cultivate high-net-worth investors, you will need to work through financial advisors and build their confidence and understanding of your capabilities. This approach has some economies of scale that can pay off for hedge funds and funds-of-funds, since a supportive advisor could theoretically recommend a single product to dozens of qualified clients. Single-family offices, however, respond to a more institutional approach since they conduct much of their own research and require institutional-quality data and information when evaluating a product. As a result, each office will need to be handled separately and treated with special care in order for you to win its approval.

However, as affluent investors consider their many options, the odds are good that more than one prospective firm will measure up in terms of its investment strategy and also get the stamp of approval from the investors' advisors. At that stage, the clincher can be "Storywork," the business of crafting highly customized and (ideally) captivating marketing messages that will resonate with affluent investors.

SWITCHING
BEHAVIOR

WE'VE NOW DISCUSSED THE WAYS THAT affluent hedge fund and fund-of-funds investors find products to invest in as well as the criteria they use to evaluate the options available to them and select one product over another. In this chapter, we will examine data that relates to the dynamics that cause affluent investors to switch from one fund to another. We will also identify the reasons that affluent investors choose to sell their hedge funds and funds-of-funds as well as the significance of those reasons to the firms the investors are leaving.

In our research, we found that fewer than one in five hedge fund or fund-of-funds investors had liquidated their position in one fund for another within the previous year. This turnover rate is far lower than that of more mainstream products such as mutual funds, but nonetheless high enough to warrant attention, especially given the amount of money involved (Exhibit 5.1). Further, we found that there was no statistically meaningful difference in the percentage of investors that switched by demographic segment (Exhibit 5.2).

EXHIBIT 5.1:

SWITCHED FROM ONE HEDGE FUND OR FUND-OF-FUNDS TO ANOTHER IN THE PRECEDING YEAR
N = 428 AFFLUENT INVESTORS

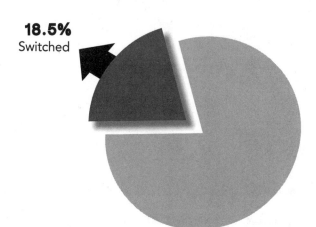

18.5%
Switched

EXHIBIT 5.2:

SWITCHED BY DEMOGRAPHIC SEGMENTS
N = 428 AFFLUENT INVESTORS

18.1%   **19.0%**

High-net-worth   Single-family offices

SWITCHING BY
BEHAVIORAL SEGMENT

A somewhat more pronounced difference was revealed when the switching data was viewed by behavioral segments, with more than twice as many Evaluators saying they had moved from one fund to another in the past year (Exhibit 5.3). This is not a revelatory finding as we know that Evaluators are more interested and involved in the investing process and conduct much of their own research, but firms should nonetheless understand the drivers behind this behavior so they can manage potential client defections more proactively.

EXHIBIT 5.3:
SWITCHED BY BEHAVIORAL SEGMENTS
N = 428 AFFLUENT INVESTORS

26.3%

11.0%

Delegators   Evaluators

71

REASONS FOR
SWITCHING

When affluent investors decided to get out of a hedge fund or fund-of-funds, the majority admitted to relying on their gut instinct. More than half, 57 percent, simply said that a "bad feeling" was the most important reason for switching (Exhibit 5.4). When we constructed a causal model with this "bad feeling" as the dependent variable, we found that it was – in many ways – the aggregate of all of the negative factors coupled with the hedge fund or fund-of-funds firm being "distant" and unresponsive.

The next most frequently cited reason, mentioned by 55.7 percent of the respondents, was a lack of responsiveness from the hedge fund or fund-of-funds professionals with whom they had invested. Given the high-touch service most affluent individuals demand and receive from the various professionals they rely on for expertise, it stands to reason that they would expect similar treatment from their investment relationships, especially given the amount of money involved, and take steps to remedy the situation if such high-touch service was lacking.

A comparable number, 54.4 percent, said their decision to leave a particular fund was prompted by an advisor's recommendation. When we work with very high-end professional advisors, we regularly see the influence they have with their wealthy clientele. This position of authority is a product of their expertise coupled with their finely tuned relationship management skills. As such, their ability to direct their wealthy clients when it comes to investing is not in question.

Performance, one of the most important reasons to invest in the first place, was cited as the reason for switching by only 40.5 percent of the survey respondents. Since performance is typically the direct result of the philosophies and actions of the portfolio manager, it makes sense that 39.2 percent of investors cited turnover in the hedge fund's or fund-of-funds' management team as their reason for switching funds.

Very few investors felt that changes to a fund's features, such as hurdle rates and lock-up periods, were significant enough reasons for them to switch to a different fund, and none of our respondents said a change in ownership structure was behind their decision to sell – additional proof that investors understand and tolerate the transitional aspects of the hedge fund industry.

EXHIBIT 5.4:
"VERY" OR "EXTREMELY" IMPORTANT
REASONS TO CHANGE
N = 79 AFFLUENT INVESTORS

REASON	TOTAL
A "bad" feeling	57.0%
The professionals at the hedge fund or fund-of-funds firms were unresponsive	55.7%
The recommendation of a professional advisor	54.4%
Uncomfortable with the investment approach or strategy of the manager	41.8%
Poor investment performance	40.5%
Change in managers or key staff at the hedge fund or fund-of-funds firm	39.2%
The hedge fund or fund-of-funds firm deviated from the agreed-upon approach or strategy	31.6%
The hedge fund or fund-of-funds proved to be too risky	16.5%
Change in investor base	11.4%
Recommendation of a business associate	7.6%
A change in your financial or personal situation	6.3%
Changes in hurdles	5.1%

73

REASON	TOTAL
Changes in lock-ups	**2.5%**
Questionable behavior by the professionals at the hedge fund or fund-of-funds firm	**1.3%**
Recommendation of a friend or family member	**0.0%**
The sale of the hedge fund or fund-of-funds firm to a financial services firm	**0.0%**
The sale of the hedge fund or fund-of-funds firm to another hedge fund or fund-of-funds boutique firm	**0.0%**

74

CONCLUSIONS

There are some important takeaways for hedge fund and fund-of-funds professionals in this data. While you certainly can't anticipate or explain away an investor's bad vibes about a product, there are steps you can take to ensure that your investors have the information they need from you and your fund about their investment so that their emotional reactions are muted. At the same time, you can benefit from the "gut feeling effect" by creating an overall experience that is positive for the affluent investor.

Similarly, while strong performance is never a guarantee (nor, for that matter, something over which you have complete control), you do have complete control over, and can guarantee, responsive client service. Staying in front of your affluent clients (and their advisors), both proactively and reactively, can help to all but eliminate any concerns they may have about your commitment to them and their assets.

Financial advisors, like individual investors, will also need your attention in order to stabilize their affluent clients. They will evaluate products and results on an ongoing basis for their clients and expect your cooperation and responsiveness to help them do their job. A lack of communication or information will make it easier for those advisors to recommend that their clients leave when your fund's performance is lower than expected. Conversely, a collaborative process will be appreciated and remembered and can engender the faith and goodwill needed to placate restless or nervous affluent clients during a volatile quarter or two. In sum, in this highly competitive environment, neither performance nor high-touch service alone is enough to retain wealthy clients and stop them from switching; you must deliver both.

THE IMPORTANCE OF
SATISFACTION

6

IN THE LAST CHAPTER, WE DISCUSSED THE MANY reasons that wealthy investors sell the hedge funds in their portfolios. The most commonly cited reason was a "bad feeling," which can be frustratingly nebulous for the hedge fund and fund-of-funds professionals who want real insight into the switching behavior of their investors. Our perspective, based on years of studying and working with wealthy individuals and backed by the findings in the previous chapter, is that satisfaction plays a significant and influential role in how affluent investors perceive and handle their portfolios. As a result, we asked our survey participants a series of follow-up questions about their level of satisfaction with the hedge fund or fund-of-funds firms that had the largest percentage of their investable assets. These questions allowed us to closely examine and assess the relationship between investment performance and satisfaction, and how those issues will color an affluent investor's willingness to invest more money or refer new business, two actions that make good clients invaluable.

SATISFACTION

First the good news: A healthy majority of the hedge fund and fund-of-funds investors we surveyed, 70.6 percent, characterized themselves as "highly satisfied" with their largest hedge fund or fund-of-funds holding (Exhibit 6.1). Of course, that means there was nonetheless a not insignificant group of dissatisfied investors that may be at risk if their concerns are not actively addressed.

80

EXHIBIT 6.1:
OVERALL SATISFACTION
N = 428 AFFLUENT INVESTORS

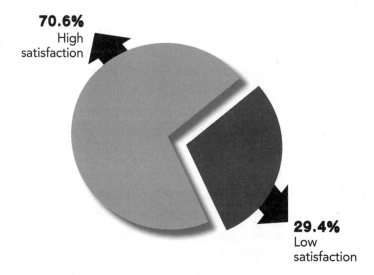

70.6%
High
satisfaction

29.4%
Low
satisfaction

When we view the satisfaction levels by demographic segment, the percentages remained fairly constant, but there were slightly fewer satisfied single-family offices (Exhibit 6.2). Behaviorally, however, the results were very different. The percentage of Delegators with high satisfaction was much higher, at 81.3 percent, than the percentage of Evaluators who felt the same way, just 59.3 percent (Exhibit 6.3). As most Evaluators are professional investors, they are more likely to know how the fund is performing at any given time and be more critical in their assessment of the results. Delegators, in contrast, usually depend on their advisors for product-specific information, and frequently their satisfaction level – high or low – is directly related to the quality of the interactions and communications they have with their advisor, not the hedge fund or fund-of-funds firm itself.

EXHIBIT 6.2:

OVERALL SATISFACTION BY DEMOGRAPHIC SEGMENTS
N = 428 AFFLUENT INVESTORS

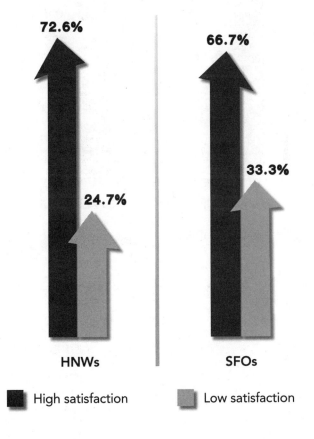

EXHIBIT 6.3:

# OVERALL SATISFACTION BY BEHAVIORAL SEGMENTS
N = 428 AFFLUENT INVESTORS

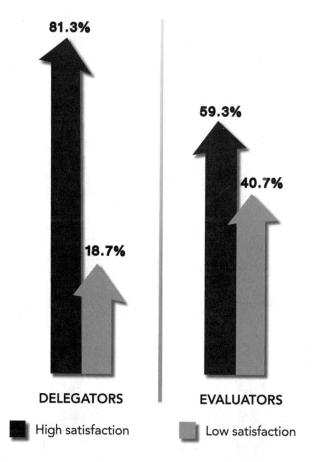

82

DELEGATORS **EVALUATORS**

■ High satisfaction ■ Low satisfaction

PERFORMANCE
EXPERIENCE

Next, we asked the respondents to indicate how their largest hedge fund or fund-of-funds investment performed relative to their expectations. In this case, slightly more than half said their fund performed as expected, 20.1 percent said the performance was better than expected, and roughly a quarter said the performance was worse than expected (Exhibit 6.4).

EXHIBIT 6.4:

INVESTMENT PERFORMANCE
COMPARED TO EXPECTATIONS
N = 428 AFFLUENT INVESTORS

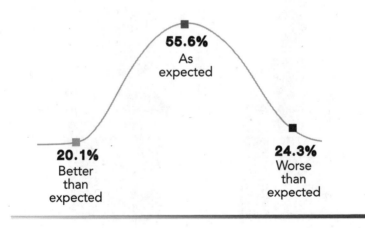

55.6%
As
expected

20.1%
Better
than
expected

24.3%
Worse
than
expected

83

Again, additional insights were revealed by further analyzing the responses of each investor segment. The majority of both demographic segments said their funds performed as expected (Exhibit 6.5). However, just 16.4 percent of wealthy individuals said their performance was better compared to 27.2 percent of single-family offices. Behaviorally speaking, about 20 percent of both segments said their performance was better than expected (Exhibit 6.6). About two-thirds of Delegators said it was what they expected with just 16.4 percent saying it was worse. Less than half, 47.8 percent, of Evaluators got what they expected when it came to performance, and one-third said the performance was worse.

EXHIBIT 6.5:

INVESTMENT PERFORMANCE COMPARED TO
EXPECTATIONS BY DEMOGRAPHIC SEGMENTS
N = 428 AFFLUENT INVESTORS

84

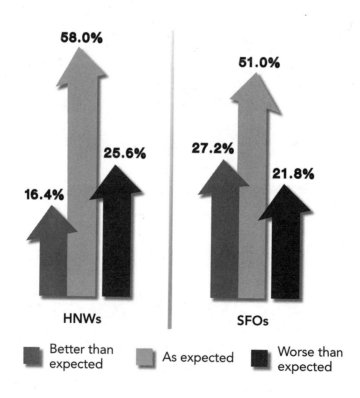

HNWs   SFOs

Better than expected   As expected   Worse than expected

EXHIBIT 6.6:

INVESTMENT PERFORMANCE COMPARED TO EXPECTATIONS BY BEHAVIORAL SEGMENTS
N = 428 AFFLUENT INVESTORS

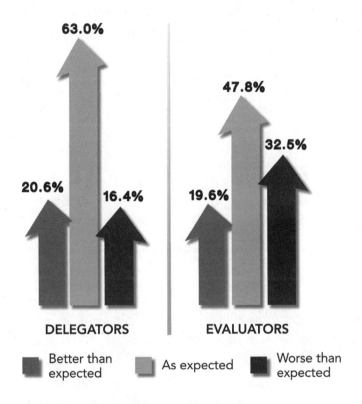

63.0%

47.8%

32.5%

20.6%

16.4%

19.6%

DELEGATORS

EVALUATORS

■ Better than expected   ■ As expected   ■ Worse than expected

PERFORMANCE AND
SATISFACTION

The following charts provide insight into the impact that performance can have on an investor's satisfaction level. For those investors who described themselves as "highly satisfied," more than half said their performance was as expected, roughly one-quarter said it was better than expected, and just 17.5 percent said it was worse than expected (Exhibit 6.7). To summarize, 82.5 percent of highly satisfied investors got what they expected, or more, from their hedge fund investment.

EXHIBIT 6.7:

INVESTMENT PERFORMANCE COMPARED TO EXPECTATIONS BY **HIGH SATISFACTION**

N = 302 AFFLUENT INVESTORS

56.3%
As
expected

26.2%
Better
than expected

17.5%
Worse
than expected

86

Still focusing on highly satisfied investors, we then viewed the results by demographic segments. This time, an even larger percentage of high-net-worth individuals, 61.8 percent, said their fund's performance was in line with their expectations while the remaining 38.2 percent were evenly split between better or worse than expected (Exhibit 6.8). Single-family offices broke down very differently, with 40.8 percent claiming better performance than anticipated, 44.9 percent saying that performance met expectations, and just 14.3 percent saying it fell short.

Given the institutional nature of the investment process at most single-family offices, having a product perform as intended is mandatory, but it will not necessarily translate into client satisfaction. The upside surprise regarding performance, however, may have a favorable influence on how a product is perceived and on the overall relationship between the single-family office and the fund firm.

EXHIBIT 6.8:

INVESTMENT PERFORMANCE COMPARED TO
EXPECTATIONS BY **HIGH SATISFACTION** BY
DEMOGRAPHIC SEGMENTS
N = 302 AFFLUENT INVESTORS

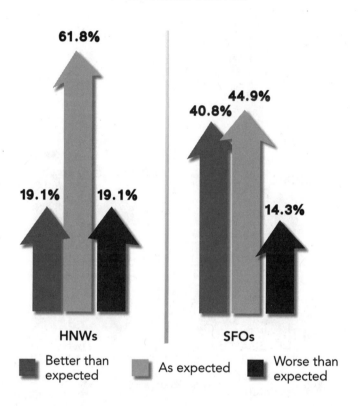

For the majority of Delegators, 69.1 percent, their investment performance was as expected. For about a quarter of them it was better and for only 7.3 percent was it worse (Exhibit 6.9). Meanwhile, the investment performance was fairly evenly distributed for Evaluators.

EXHIBIT 6.9:

INVESTMENT PERFORMANCE COMPARED TO EXPECTATIONS BY **HIGH SATISFACTION** BY BEHAVIORAL SEGMENTS

N = 302 AFFLUENT INVESTORS

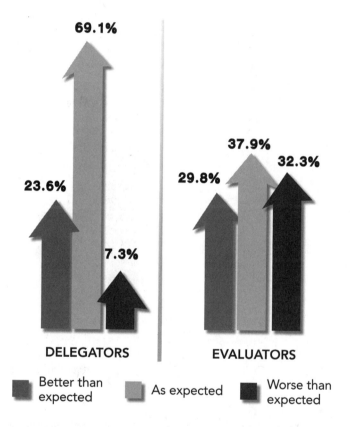

	DELEGATORS	EVALUATORS
69.1% (As expected)		
23.6% (Better than expected)		
7.3% (Worse than expected)		
29.8% (Better than expected)		
37.9% (As expected)		
32.3% (Worse than expected)		

■ Better than expected ■ As expected ■ Worse than expected

88

The charts above indicate that high-net-worth investors and Delegators gain a certain degree of satisfaction from having their hedge funds simply deliver against expectations. What's also important to note is the fact that there's generally an intermediary between the fund firms and these affluent clients. The financial advisors – presuming they're good at relating to the wealthy – are constantly working to manage the expectations of their clients. By contrast, meeting expectations is a condition for doing business with single-family offices and those kinds of results do not have as great an effect on their satisfaction.

THE OTHER END OF
THE SPECTRUM

We then looked at the same data for affluent investors who were less satisfied with their biggest hedge fund or fund-of-funds investment. Not surprisingly, only 5.6 percent of the total group said performance was better than expected and a whopping 40.4 percent said it was worse – more than twice the number of highly satisfied investors with performance that was below expectations (Exhibit 6.10). Clearly, products that don't meet expectations play a role in investor satisfaction and must be offset by other factors such as client relationship management in order to retain wealthy clients. (Relationship management is discussed in greater detail in the next chapter.)

EXHIBIT 6.10:
INVESTMENT PERFORMANCE COMPARED TO
EXPECTATIONS BY **LOW SATISFACTION**
N = 126 AFFLUENT INVESTORS

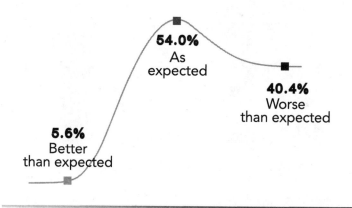

54.0%
As
expected

40.4%
Worse
than expected

5.6%
Better
than expected

When viewed by demographic segment, the more rigorous and investment savvy nature of single-family offices became crystal clear: About two-thirds said the performance of their fund met their expectations, 36.7 percent said it was worse, and not one claimed that the fund's performance exceeded their projections (Exhibit 6.11). High-net-worth investors were less stringent than their single-family office counterparts, but their satisfaction was evidently still influenced by their performance experience as 42.8 percent said their fund performed lower than expected.

EXHIBIT 6.11:
INVESTMENT PERFORMANCE COMPARED TO
EXPECTATIONS BY **LOW SATISFACTION** BY
DEMOGRAPHIC SEGMENTS
N = 126 AFFLUENT INVESTORS

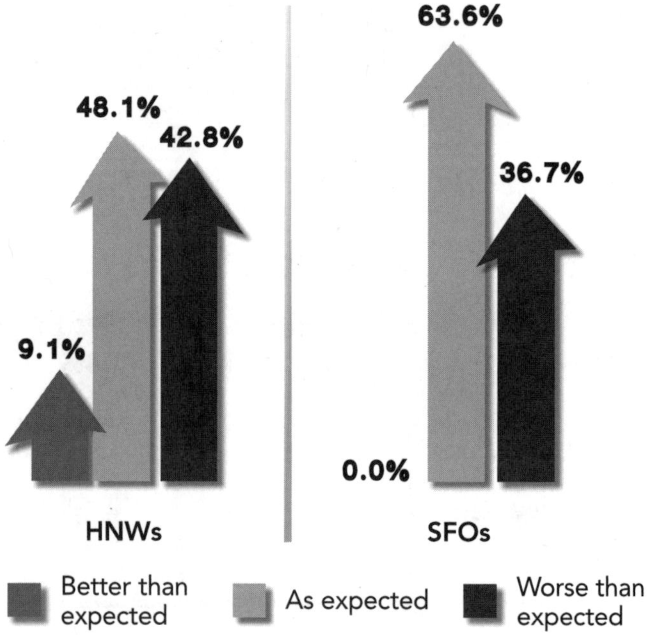

90

	HNWs	**SFOs**
Better than expected	9.1%	0.0%
As expected	48.1%	63.6%
Worse than expected	42.8%	36.7%

DELEGATORS
AND EVALUATORS

When viewed by behavioral segments, we found that more than half of the less satisfied Delegators, 56.1 percent, said their fund's performance did not meet their expectations (Exhibit 6.12). Just 36.6 percent said the fund performed as expected and only 7.3 percent said it was better than expected. A larger group of Evaluators, 62.4 percent, said their product performed as expected while 32.9 percent claimed performance was worse and just 4.7 percent said it did better than expected.

EXHIBIT 6.12:
INVESTMENT PERFORMANCE COMPARED
TO EXPECTATIONS BY **LOW SATISFACTION**
BY BEHAVIORAL SEGMENTS
N = 126 AFFLUENT INVESTORS

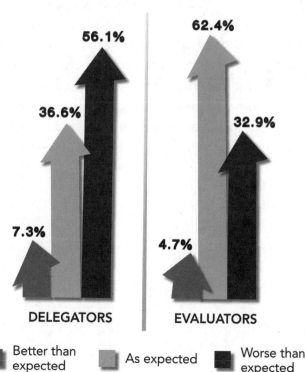

56.1%

36.6%

7.3%

62.4%

32.9%

4.7%

DELEGATORS   EVALUATORS

Better than expected   As expected   Worse than expected

91

These figures indicate that poor performance has a stronger negative influence on satisfaction for high-net-worth investors and Delegators than it does for single-family offices or Evaluators. It also indicates that simply meeting performance expectations is more likely to be perceived negatively than positively by single-family offices and Evaluators, and funds falling into that category must improve or be wrapped in other valued services in order to maintain satisfaction and retain affluent clients.

LOOKING AND
PLANNING AHEAD

An important part of investment product stability and profitability is asset retention, so we also queried our affluent survey participants about a variety of scenarios to determine how their experiences would shape their actions relative to their hedge fund or fund-of-funds firm. With consistent performance year over year, very little was likely to change, according to investors. About one-third said they would invest more money and 24.8 percent said they would talk to other advisors about the fund (Exhibit 6.13). Overall, referrals to and defections from the fund were less likely to happen in the face of solid performance.

EXHIBIT 6.13:

INVESTMENT PERFORMANCE STAYS THE SAME IN THE FORTHCOMING YEAR
N = 428 AFFLUENT INVESTORS

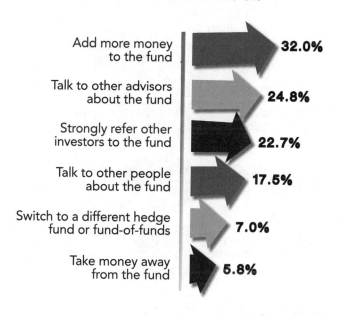

Add more money to the fund — **32.0%**

Talk to other advisors about the fund — **24.8%**

Strongly refer other investors to the fund — **22.7%**

Talk to other people about the fund — **17.5%**

Switch to a different hedge fund or fund-of-funds — **7.0%**

Take money away from the fund — **5.8%**

93

Consistent performance, however, is viewed differently depending on the satisfaction level of the client. Highly satisfied investors said they would maintain or increase their ownership stake, while about one in five of the less satisfied investors said they would take some or all of their assets out of the fund if performance stayed the same (Exhibit 6.14). Performance also variously impacted their willingness to discuss or refer the fund to professionals, peers, or clients.

EXHIBIT 6.14:

INVESTMENT PERFORMANCE STAYS THE SAME IN THE FORTHCOMING YEAR BY SATISFACTION

N = 428 AFFLUENT INVESTORS

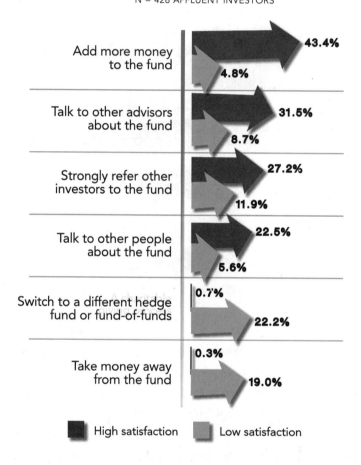

Add more money to the fund — 43.4% / 4.8%

Talk to other advisors about the fund — 31.5% / 8.7%

Strongly refer other investors to the fund — 27.2% / 11.9%

Talk to other people about the fund — 22.5% / 5.6%

Switch to a different hedge fund or fund-of-funds — 0.7% / 22.2%

Take money away from the fund — 0.3% / 19.0%

High satisfaction   Low satisfaction

The following chart shows the actions highly satisfied affluent individuals and single-family offices would take over the next year if performance remained consistent, and both demographic segments said they would maintain their positions in the fund. Almost half of the individual investors, 45.1 percent, said they would consider increasing the size of their investment (Exhibit 6.15). Under the same conditions, 39.8 percent of single-family offices would increase their investment, 36.7 percent would mention the product to other professionals, 41.8 percent would endorse the product to other investors, and 45.9 percent would discuss it in a variety of professional contexts – figures that reinforce the importance of consistency to institutional-style investors.

EXHIBIT 6.15:

INVESTMENT PERFORMANCE STAYS THE SAME IN THE FORTHCOMING YEAR BY **HIGH SATISFACTION** AND DEMOGRAPHIC SEGMENTS

N = 302 AFFLUENT INVESTORS

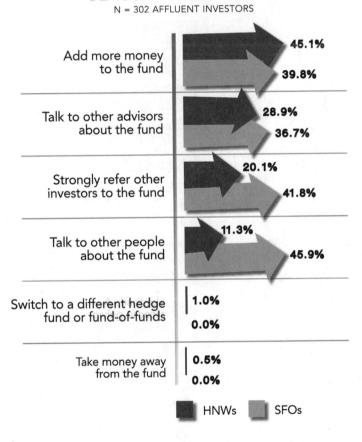

	HNWs	SFOs
Add more money to the fund	45.1%	39.8%
Talk to other advisors about the fund	28.9%	36.7%
Strongly refer other investors to the fund	20.1%	41.8%
Talk to other people about the fund	11.3%	45.9%
Switch to a different hedge fund or fund-of-funds	1.0%	0.0%
Take money away from the fund	0.5%	0.0%

95

High-net-worth investors with low satisfaction were far more likely to take action than single-family offices in a similar situation. In fact, almost one-quarter said they would decrease their investment and about one-third would find another fund to invest in if performance did not change (Exhibit 6.16). Despite their low satisfaction, single-family offices were not likely to take any action if performance remained the same – an approach that allowed them to meet with and monitor the management team and the fund, although 12.2 percent said they would consider reducing their total investment.

EXHIBIT 6.16:

INVESTMENT PERFORMANCE STAYS THE SAME IN THE FORTHCOMING YEAR BY **LOW SATISFACTION** AND DEMOGRAPHIC SEGMENTS

N = 126 AFFLUENT INVESTORS

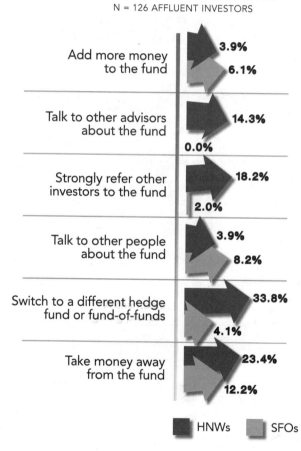

	HNWs	SFOs
Add more money to the fund	3.9%	6.1%
Talk to other advisors about the fund	14.3%	0.0%
Strongly refer other investors to the fund	18.2%	2.0%
Talk to other people about the fund	3.9%	8.2%
Switch to a different hedge fund or fund-of-funds	33.8%	4.1%
Take money away from the fund	23.4%	12.2%

ACTIONS BY
BEHAVIORAL SEGMENT

From a behavioral standpoint, the combination of consistent performance and high satisfaction engendered different results. Half of the highly satisfied Delegators said they would add more money to the fund if investment performance was consistent, but they were less inclined to take any other action (Exhibit 6.17). Highly satisfied Evaluators, however, said they would readily talk to their network of advisors and peers about the product when it delivered consistent results, and about one-third said they would consider increasing their investment.

EXHIBIT 6.17:

INVESTMENT PERFORMANCE STAYS THE SAME IN THE FORTHCOMING YEAR BY **HIGH SATISFACTION** AND BEHAVIORAL SEGMENTS

N = 302 AFFLUENT INVESTORS

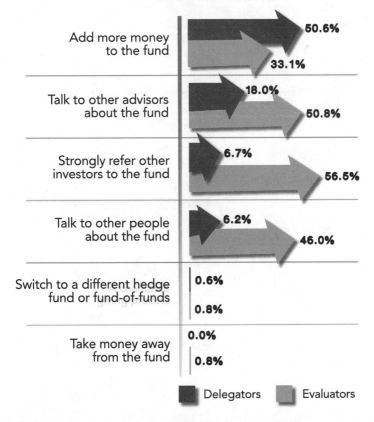

	Delegators	Evaluators
Add more money to the fund	50.6%	33.1%
Talk to other advisors about the fund	18.0%	50.8%
Strongly refer other investors to the fund	6.7%	56.5%
Talk to other people about the fund	6.2%	46.0%
Switch to a different hedge fund or fund-of-funds	0.6%	0.8%
Take money away from the fund	0.0%	0.8%

Delegators   Evaluators

97

Low satisfaction levels have a similar effect on the behavioral segments, as seen below (Exhibit 6.18). Delegators were once again more likely to take action, with 43.9 percent saying they would plan to switch funds while 31.7 percent said they would take away assets in a scenario with no changes to performance results (Exhibit 6.18). Evaluators would take a more measured approach, with very few planning to take much action at all until they had assessed the situation to their satisfaction.

EXHIBIT 6.18:

INVESTMENT PERFORMANCE STAYS THE SAME IN THE FORTHCOMING YEAR BY **LOW SATISFACTION** AND BEHAVIORAL SEGMENTS

N = 126 AFFLUENT INVESTORS

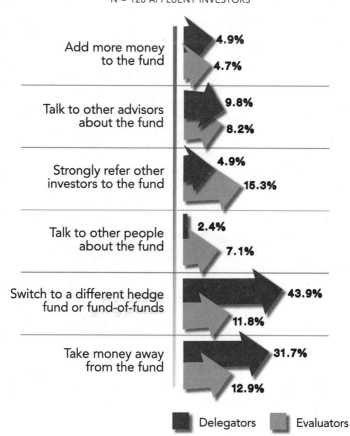

	Delegators	Evaluators
Add more money to the fund	4.9%	4.7%
Talk to other advisors about the fund	9.8%	8.2%
Strongly refer other investors to the fund	4.9%	15.3%
Talk to other people about the fund	2.4%	7.1%
Switch to a different hedge fund or fund-of-funds	43.9%	11.8%
Take money away from the fund	31.7%	12.9%

CONCLUSIONS

Understanding your affluent clients can be a complicated task – and one that becomes even more complicated when you begin to dissect their satisfaction levels and personal experiences, the relationship between the two, and what influence that relationship has on the future stability of the broader client and firm relationship. Clearly, and not surprisingly, satisfaction plays a big role in an investor's willingness to stick with a product. And, again not surprisingly, hitting or exceeding performance targets played an important role in client satisfaction.

It's important to keep in mind the fact that individuals were more appreciative of a firm's meeting its investment expectations than were single-family offices. However, high-net-worth investors were also more likely to act rashly when they were displeased, whereas single-family offices tended to be less emotionally reactive and relatively more deliberate. In sum, while there is an undeniable correlation between performance and satisfaction, there are other factors that can play a key role in satisfaction – factors that will be detailed in the next chapter – and those actions should not be overlooked if your goal is to find and keep affluent clients.

CREATING HIGHLY
SATISFIED
AFFLUENT INVESTORS

WHILE **INVESTMENT PERFORMANCE UNDER-** standably plays the most significant role in affluent client satisfaction, there are other aspects of a client's experience with a hedge fund or fund-of-funds firm that can meaningfully impact his or her overall level of satisfaction. We base this conclusion on our first-hand research and our extensive in-the-field experience consulting with the private wealth market. In fact, as important as investment performance is, we have found that it's possible to achieve high levels of affluent client satisfaction even when that investment performance falls off. The operative word here, however, is "possible," because very few firms in the investment world emphasize these non-performance client services, despite the very clear benefits, which include helping firms to hold onto clients during downturns, attracting new clients through referrals, and getting additional assets from existing clients.

Over the years, we have empirically identified 24 activities that hedge fund or fund-of-funds firms might undertake as part of their client service efforts, and we asked our study participants if the hedge fund or fund-of-funds firm with the greatest percentage of their investable assets had provided similar

103

services to them. Surprisingly, we found that, despite the basic nature of many of these activities, very few affluent clients had been on the receiving end. In fact, only about one-third of the respondents said their fund firm spent the time required to address their questions and explain their products, provided updates on the market environment, discussed the role the fund plays in their portfolio, and delivered timely information and written materials (Exhibit 7.1). All other activities were experienced by even fewer affluent clients; for instance, just 18.9 percent said they received proactive contact from their hedge fund or fund-of-funds firm, and only 7.7 percent said their fund firm introduced new ways to achieve better returns with the products they offered.

RELATIONSHIP
BUILDING

Given the near exclusive focus on investing at most hedge fund and fund-of-funds firms and the highly specialized strategies of many funds, it's perhaps not surprising to find that a mere 12.9 percent of clients spoke with their firms about non-investment interests and less than one percent received other financial plans, products, and services from the hedge funds or funds-of-funds they invested with. In sum, most fund firms have relied exclusively on their investment expertise as the way to attract and retain affluent clients and have overlooked the client-focused activities that can strengthen relationships, bypassing a potential opportunity for establishing a competitive advantage in an increasingly crowded marketplace.

EXHIBIT 7.1:

# RELATIONSHIP BUILDING ACTIONS
N = 428 AFFLUENT INVESTORS

Spent as much time as necessary explaining concepts and/or answering your questions	**35.3%**
Provided their perspectives on the economy and/or markets	**33.2%**
Regularly discussed with you how their fund fits into your portfolio	**32.0%**
Provided timely information	**31.8%**
Provided substantial written material	**30.1%**
Regularly discussed with you their investment approach or strategy	**28.5%**
Discussed your other investments	**26.9%**
Asked you if you wanted anything explained to you	**21.5%**
Were able to explain complex concepts in an easy-to-understand way	**19.9%**
Were very patient while providing explanations	**19.2%**
Contacted you and provided perspective and insights when dramatic economic or political changes occurred	**18.9%**
Encouraged you to express your preferences about what you would like to discuss	**18.5%**
Encouraged you to openly express your opinions	**18.5%**
Encouraged you to ask questions freely	**18.2%**
Understood what was "really" important to you	**16.6%**
Encouraged you to meet with them often	**16.1%**
Discussed your goals, concerns, and interests outside of investing	**12.9%**
Discussed ways you can generate a better return using their fund	**7.7%**

Kept you aware of any complications or problems at the fund	**7.5%**
Encouraged you to suggest ways to improve operations and service	**5.8%**
Introduced you to qualified experts in other areas	**3.5%**
Introduced you to other money managers	**0.9%**
Provided you with non-financial or planning services	**0.2%**
Provided you with other types of financial services or products	**0.0%**

106

SATISFACTION
LEVELS

Despite the relatively low incidence of these client service efforts, in this environment, we wanted to understand whether some activities had a more influential role than others in generating satisfaction. The following table shows the difference between the experiences of highly satisfied affluent investors and less satisfied investors, and, in every case, less satisfied investors were less likely to have received any such services (Exhibit 7.2). In fact, 15 of the 24 actions weren't provided to a single individual with low satisfaction, and another four were provided to less than 2 percent of the group. When we consider these findings in the context of all the research on satisfaction we've conducted with affluent investors over 20 years, we see that – in general – most hedge funds and funds-of-funds have limited their client relationship management efforts to the bare minimum. It also underscores the role other forms of client interaction can play in building affluent client relationships and engendering satisfaction. In short, key opportunities to profitably bond with clients are being overlooked, again and again.

EXHIBIT 7.2:

RELATIONSHIP BUILDING ACTIONS BY SATISFACTION
N = 428 AFFLUENT INVESTORS

ACTION	HIGH SATISFACTION	LOW SATISFACTION
Spent as much time as necessary explaining concepts and/or answering your questions	37.4%	30.2%
Provided their perspectives on the economy and/or markets	37.1%	23.8%
Regularly discussed with you how their fund fits into your portfolio	32.5%	31.0%
Provided timely information	33.8%	27.0%
Provided substantial written material	35.4%	17.5%
Regularly discussed with you their investment approach or strategy	33.1%	17.5%
Discussed your other investments	30.5%	18.3%
Asked you if you wanted anything explained to you	30.5%	0.0%
Were able to explain complex concepts in an easy-to-understand way	28.1%	0.0%
Were very patient while providing explanations	26.2%	2.4%
Contacted you and provided perspective and insights when dramatic economic or political changes occurred	26.8%	0.0%
Encouraged you to express your preferences about what you would like to discuss	26.2%	0.0%
Encouraged you to openly express your opinions	25.8%	0.8%

107

ACTION	HIGH SATISFACTION	LOW SATISFACTION
Encouraged you to ask questions freely	25.5%	0.8%
Understood what was "really" important to you	22.8%	1.6%
Encouraged you to meet with them often	22.8%	0.0%
Discussed your goals, concerns, and interests outside of investing	18.2%	0.0%
Discussed ways you can generate a better return using their fund	10.9%	0.0%
Kept you aware of any complications or problems at the fund	10.6%	0.0%
Encouraged you to suggest ways to improve operations and service	8.3%	0.0%
Introduced you to qualified experts in other areas	5.0%	0.0%
Introduced you to other money managers	1.3%	0.0%
Provided you with non-financial or planning services	0.3%	0.0%
Provided you with other types of financial services or products	0.0%	0.0%

THE DEMOGRAPHIC
BREAKDOWN

By looking at the demographic breakdown within the universe of highly satisfied investors, we were able to identify which activities were most important to high-net-worth individuals as well as those that mattered most to single-family offices. In every scenario, single-family offices received a higher, in some cases much higher, level of service from the fund firm (Exhibit

7.3). This is not surprising as many institutional investors take an active role in managing their sub-advisory relationships and individuals generally rely on their financial advisors to intercede for them.

EXHIBIT 7.3:
RELATIONSHIP BUILDING ACTIONS BY
HIGH SATISFACTION AND DEMOGRAPHIC SEGMENTS
N = 302 AFFLUENT INVESTORS

ACTION	HNWs	SFOs
Spent as much time as necessary explaining concepts and/or answering your questions	20.1%	73.5%
Provided their perspectives on the economy and/or markets	17.6%	77.6%
Provided substantial written material	20.1%	67.3%
Provided timely information	15.7%	71.4%
Regularly discussed with you their investment approach or strategy	20.6%	59.2%
Regularly discussed with you how their fund fits into your portfolio	11.8%	75.5%
Asked you if you wanted anything explained to you	21.1%	50.0%
Discussed your other investments	10.8%	71.4%
Were able to explain complex concepts in an easy-to-understand way	19.6%	45.9%
Contacted you and provided perspectiveand insights when dramatic economic or political changes occurred	21.1%	38.8%
Encouraged you to express your preferences about what you would like to discuss	17.2%	44.9%
Were very patient while providing explanations	20.1%	38.8%

109

ACTION	HNWs	SFOs
Encouraged you to openly express your opinions	18.1%	41.8%
Encouraged you to ask questions freely	18.1%	40.8%
Encouraged you to meet with them often	9.3%	51.0%
Understood what was "really" important to you	11.3%	46.9%
Discussed your goals, concerns, and interests outside of investing	12.7%	29.6%
Discussed ways you can generate a better return using their fund	2.9%	27.6%
Kept you aware of any complications or problems at the fund	5.9%	20.4%
Encouraged you to provide ways to improve operations and service	1.5%	22.4%
Introduced you to qualified experts in other areas	5.9%	3.1%
Introduced you to other money managers	0.5%	3.1%
Provided you with non-financial or planning services	0.0%	1.0%
Provided you with other types of financial services or products	0.0%	0.0%

BEHAVIORAL FEEDBACK

The following table displays the behavioral breakdown within the universe of highly satisfied investors, and the results reinforce the way that each segment prefers to operate. Not surprisingly, highly satisfied Evaluators, those investors who take an active role in the investment process, had especially high levels of interaction with the hedge funds and funds-of-funds with the greatest portion of their assets (Exhibit 7.4). Conversely, highly satisfied Delegators had almost no interaction with their hedge funds or funds-of-funds firms. In practice, hedge funds and funds-of-funds firms targeting Delegators must focus their relationship building efforts not on the affluent themselves, but on the intermediaries that are controlling where any assets are being placed.

EXHIBIT 7.4:

RELATIONSHIP BUILDING ACTIONS BY
HIGH SATISFACTION AND BEHAVIORAL SEGMENTS
N = 302 AFFLUENT INVESTORS

ACTION	DELEGATORS	EVALUATORS
Spent as much time as necessary explaining concepts and/or answering your questions	1.1%	89.5%
Provided their perspectives on the economy and/or markets	0.6%	89.5%
Provided substantial written material	2.2%	83.1%
Provided timely information	0.6%	81.5%
Regularly discussed with you their investment approach or strategy	1.1%	79.0%
Regularly discussed with you how their fund fits into your portfolio	0.0%	79.0%
Asked you if you wanted anything explained to you	1.1%	72.6%
Discussed your other investments	0.6%	73.4%
Were able to explain complex concepts in an easy-to-understand way	0.0%	68.5%

ACTION	DELEGATORS	EVALUATORS
Contacted you and provided perspective and insights when dramatic economic or political changes occurred	1.7%	62.9%
Encouraged you to express your preferences about what you would like to discuss	0.0%	63.7%
Were very patient while providing explanations	1.1%	62.1%
Encouraged you to openly express your opinions	0.0%	62.9%
Encouraged you to ask questions freely	0.0%	62.1%
Encouraged you to meet with them often	0.0%	55.6%
Understood what was "really" important to you	0.0%	55.6%
Discussed your goals, concerns, and interests outside of investing	0.0%	44.4%
Discussed ways you can generate a better return using their fund	0.0%	26.6%
Kept you aware of any complications or problems at the fund	0.0%	25.8%
Encouraged you to provide ways to improve operations and service	0.0%	20.2%
Introduced you to qualified experts in other areas	0.0%	12.1%
Introduced you to other money managers	0.6%	2.4%
Provided you with non-financial or planning services	0.6%	0.0%
Provided you with other types of financial services or products	0.0%	0.0%

112

COMMUNICATION

We also know that wealthy individuals respond most favorably when the financial professionals and firms to whom they entrust their assets take the time to determine the best way to communicate with them. For instance, some wealthy clients make quick decisions while others need time to ruminate and solicit additional opinions. Some wealthy clients prefer the "big picture" and others like to understand the details of every situation. Some prefer e-mail and others expect to meet face-to-face. When you know these things about your affluent clients, you can adjust the way you deal with them to accommodate their preferences and thereby increase their level of comfort and satisfaction.

To that end, we asked the hedge fund and fund-of-funds investors in our study to identify the methods of communication they found most valuable, and more than three-quarters of the respondents cited their advisors or investment consultants as the primary go-between and the most effective way of communicating with them (Exhibit 7.5). Other methods were deemed far less relevant, with 38.8 percent citing written reports, 29.2 percent preferring in-person meetings, and a similar percentage favoring e-mail. Memo to AT&T: Only 4.7 percent felt the phone was the best way to communicate with their largest hedge fund or fund-of-funds relationship.

113

EXHIBIT 7.5:
"VERY" OR "EXTREMELY" IMPORTANT MEANS OF COMMUNICATING
N = 428 AFFLUENT INVESTORS

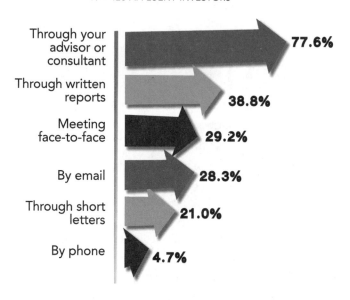

Through your advisor or consultant	77.6%
Through written reports	38.8%
Meeting face-to-face	29.2%
By email	28.3%
Through short letters	21.0%
By phone	4.7%

114

Since most high-net-worth individuals that invest in hedge funds and funds-of-funds have done so through their financial advisor, it's logical that 86.8 percent of them cited their advisor as the most important conduit for communicating about their investment and that they were, overall, far less interested in other methods of communication (Exhibit 7.6). Single-family offices, however, cited several methods of communication as important. More than half of single-family offices felt that communication through both their investment consultant and directly with the hedge fund or fund-of-funds firm were necessary, and 45.6 percent wanted written reports delivered electronically.

EXHIBIT 7.6:

"VERY" OR "EXTREMELY" IMPORTANT MEANS OF COMMUNICATING BY DEMOGRAPHIC SEGMENTS

N = 428 AFFLUENT INVESTORS

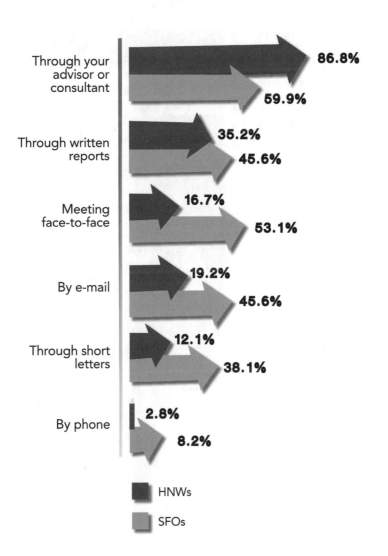

Through your advisor or consultant — 86.8% / 59.9%

Through written reports — 35.2% / 45.6%

Meeting face-to-face — 16.7% / 53.1%

By e-mail — 19.2% / 45.6%

Through short letters — 12.1% / 38.1%

By phone — 2.8% / 8.2%

HNWs
SFOs

115

THE BEHAVIORAL
BREAKDOWN

As we've seen previously, the responses from the behavioral segments echo those from the demographic segments in many ways yet still reveal very clear preferences that can shape firm and client interactions. Almost all of the Delegators, 99.1 percent, felt the most important way of interacting with their hedge fund or fund-of-funds firms was through their advisors, a finding that is consistent with this segment's desire to completely outsource their investment decision making (Exhibit 7.7). And since Evaluators prefer to conduct their own research and analysis, it also makes sense that almost 60 percent wanted a combination of reports, e-mails, and meetings as part of the process. A third-party opinion from an investment consultant was also cited by 55 percent of Evaluators, who would consider it alongside the other data they have gathered.

EXHIBIT 7.7:

"VERY" OR "EXTREMELY" IMPORTANT MEANS OF COMMUNICATING BY BEHAVIORAL SEGMENTS
N = 428 AFFLUENT INVESTORS

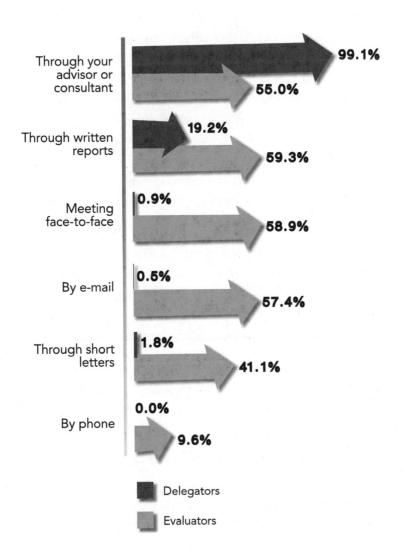

Through your advisor or consultant — 99.1% / 55.0%

Through written reports — 19.2% / 59.3%

Meeting face-to-face — 0.9% / 58.9%

By e-mail — 0.5% / 57.4%

Through short letters — 1.8% / 41.1%

By phone — 0.0% / 9.6%

Delegators

Evaluators

117

CUSTOMIZED RELATIONSHIP MANAGEMENT ACTION PLANS

Despite the evident lack of effort, creating highly satisfied affluent investors should be very important for many hedge funds and funds-of-funds. Satisfied affluent investors will stay with you during investment rough spots. They are also a source – directly and through referrals – of more monies for you to manage. In this chapter we reviewed various actions you can take to create highly satisfied affluent investors. In our recent experience many firms are indeed implementing, or trying to implement, some of these actions. At the same time, even when a firm is working in this way, it's often a scattershot rather than a systematic process.

In coaching high-end professional advisors focused on the ultra-wealthy, we have found developing customized action plans by client increases the likelihood of delivering a satisfying client experience. These are individualized sets of activities that act as a blueprint for continual follow-up between advisors and specific affluent investors.

To do this, firms need to first create a detailed relationship file for each of their important affluent investors which includes the following information:

▸▸ What was the initial means of access to the affluent investor?

▸▸ How much do they have invested in your fund compared to their other investments, including other hedge funds and funds-of-funds?

>> What is the role of your fund in their overall investment portfolio?

>> What has their experience been with hedge funds and funds-of-funds in general?

>> To date, what has been their experience with your fund in particular?

>> What story elements are most appealing to them?

>> How do they view your investment performance?

>> How many referrals have they provided you and what is their potential for future referrals?

With these answers (and more) in hand, you then need to construct a plan detailing the actions you will be taking, and when. For example, while flexibility is required, we find that pre-set dates for contacts and other client-focused initiatives can be very useful. In the end, your ability to choreograph this process will translate into a more successful endeavor and more highly-satisfied clients.

119

CONCLUSIONS

Performance results will remain the deciding factor for most hedge fund and fund-of-funds investors, but those results can clearly be bolstered by other non-investment activities. The client satisfaction that comes from strong performance can be further reinforced with relationship building activities and regular interaction. Conversely, those same efforts can reduce or delay the negative effects that weak performance can have on satisfaction. As the hedge fund industry continues to grow and competition for affluent investors increases, many firms will need to broaden their capabilities to deliver more than products and more than alpha to their investors.

And, despite their wealth and potential for referrals, most of the affluent investors in our survey had not had regular interaction with their primary hedge funds or funds-of-funds, illuminating an area that fund firms have historically placed little emphasis on and devoted few resources toward, in part because there were investors clamoring to get into their funds. However, those affluent investors that described themselves as highly satisfied with their primary hedge fund or fund-of-funds investment had heard from their funds more frequently and about a broader variety of topics than less satisfied investors, indicating that proactive client outreach can pay real dividends for fund firms, a priority given the number of funds that investors can now choose from.

Understanding your affluent investors' preferred methods of communication can also help your client-facing efforts be as efficient and effective as possible. Broadly speaking, hedge funds and funds-of-funds can address the service needs of their investors by ensuring that the advisory community has what it needs to represent your products to their clients and by developing the institutional-quality written and verbal communications that investment consultants and single-family offices expect. But, based on the particular expectations and demands of each client, whether that client is a high-net-worth investor or a single-family office, there is a lot that fund firms can do – and should do – to stand out in a crowded industry and to attract more affluent clients.

AFTERWORD

In the preceding pages, we have painted a portrait of the affluent individuals who invest in hedge funds and funds-of-funds. We have also offered strategies for success based on our extensive research and an informed perspective gained after 20 years of working with affluent clients and high-end investment firms and advisors.

So what now?

Some of the possible next steps have been outlined in this book, such as:

- ▸▸ Allocating greater resources and manpower to marketing;

- ▸▸ Realizing that each affluent prospect and investor has to be seen, and treated, as unique;

- ▸▸ Conducting highly targeted marketing campaigns based on detailed profiles of the demographic and behavioral segmenting of affluent investors;

- ▸▸ Appreciating that the best conduit for sourcing affluent high-net-worth investors is financial advisors;

- ▸▸ Understanding that fund firms should rethink the ways they find and partner with those financial advisors;

- ▸▸ Crafting customized marketing messages – featuring the Storywork methodology – that can be the difference-maker and distinguish firms and products in a crowded field;

- ▸▸ Strengthening ongoing relationships with affluent investors and their advisors, not least by improving the way firms communicate with them; and

- ▸▸ Knowing that while performance is paramount, carefully crafted and maintained relationships can help firms retain affluent clients during downswings.

Above all, there is the need for fund firms to realize that the industry they work in continues to evolve and that investors change right along with it. The firms that will be most successful in this transitional environment, as always, will be the ones that are most willing to adjust and adapt to the changes and shifts in the marketplace, constantly reexamining the way they do business – and reaping the rewards.

APPENDICES

APPENDIX A:
TO GET WEALTHY,
STAY CENTERED

Adapted from *Fortune's Fortress: A Primer on Wealth Preservation for Hedge Fund Professionals* by Russ Alan Prince, Edward A. Renn, Arthur A. Bavelas, and Mindy F. Rosenthal, MarHedge, 2007.

Klein raised a little more than US$150 million for his long/short healthcare hedge fund from friends, relatives, and business associates. He had cut his teeth at a leading investment bank where he was a star trader. In the first year, the new fund was up slightly more than 41 percent. For Klein, this translated into a new home, a Maserati Gransport Coupe, and a new paramour.

At about the same time, Rollins started a new long/short hedge fund focused on new technology companies, raising money from people he knew to the tune of about US$200 million. Like Klein, Rollins was an "escapee" – as he put it – from a well-regarded investment bank. In his first year, his fund was up 26 percent and he ended up with a Mercedes Benz S600 and an apartment in the city. He stayed with his wife.

The next year, things didn't go as well. Both the funds lost money, Klein's dropping about 6 percent while Rollins's lost nearly 13 percent. What they did next – how they behaved when they were not high-fliers – is what set the stage for their future success – or lack thereof.

First, let's state the obvious:

➤ When a hedge fund manager's fund is doing well, very well, he or she is often on "top of the world" – and exceptionally well compensated. When that happens, it's not unusual for certain feelings of omnipotence or invulnerability – some might call it "hubris" – to come into play. Sometimes the hedge fund manager stays centered, sometimes his or her ego gets the best of them.

➤ When a hedge fund manager's fund is not doing well, he or she often experiences severe stress. Certain feelings such as depression or extreme anxiety are not uncommon. Sometimes the hedge fund manager stays centered. Sometimes there are problems.

126

Whether up or down, when hedge fund managers stay centered, they're professionally in the best position to either continue to excel or to bounce back from adversity. However, based on our coaching and consulting work with hedge fund managers, keeping them centered is often an arduous and onerous undertaking. Now back to Klein and Rollins.

Klein did not stay centered. He did not stay focused on his unique talents and capabilities. Instead – as he would later describe it – he "freaked out." Not surprisingly, his erratic behavior severely impacted the performance of his hedge fund. That behavior included "playing hunches" outside of his areas of trading expertise in order to get back up and alienating some of his top employees, who fled the firm. Two years later, Klein's hedge fund was history. He's now living in an apartment in Westchester and commuting daily to work at a boutique investment bank in the city. He drives a very nice Volvo S60. And he has a new girlfriend.

In stark contrast, Rollins stayed centered. He concentrated on what he did uniquely well. While he said he experienced "off-the-wall stress and anxiety" as a result of the steep decline in performance, he did not "flake out." Instead, Rollins mentally reaffirmed his unique talents and, simultaneously, detailed his competency boundaries. He then worked out a plan that transferred certain core managerial responsibilities to other employees. He instituted a marketing program to manage the expectations and experiences of his investors, enabling him to keep their allegiance through the rough spot (see *Chapter 7: Creating Highly Satisfied Affluent Investors*). Of critical importance, he employed a variety of non-chemical methodologies, bio-feedback, and relaxation training to manage his stress and anxiety, enabling him to stay centered. Rollins attributes his subsequent success as a manager, and his ability to not only retain his clients but land new ones, to the fact that his response to adversity was measured and professional, not emotional and impulsive.

Today, Rollins has started to collect watches with the assistance of a renowned horologist. So far he's picked up two Vacheron Constantin's and a Caliber RM 008-V2 Tourbillion Split Seconds Choronograph. He's building a house in lower Fairfield County, Connecticut, with all the requisite amenities including the indoor/outdoor pool and state-of-the-art security systems. Rollins also has his eye on a jet. And, he's still married – to the same woman.

127

The moral of these stories is hardly surprising: The hedge fund business can be highly lucrative, highly stressful, and highly volatile – for everyone involved, clients and fund managers alike. While the public at large see the rewards such as the Maserati Gransport Coupe, the Caliber RM 008-V2 Tourbillion Split Seconds Choronograph, and the jet, people do not see the incredible amount of hard work and expertise that's behind that outsized success. Moreover, few investors can comprehend the ability of these hedge fund managers to harness and focus their unique talents. Fewer still recognize the multitude of obstacles – internal and external – to staying centered.

COACHES

Based on our experience of consulting with hedge fund managers, it's very easy for them to lose sight of their core skills and strengths when the world is caving in on them and – just as importantly – when they're soaring to new heights. When this happens, the hedge funds suffer. That's where coaches can come to the rescue.

Coaching hedge fund principals is a systematic process that results in their staying centered and focused on their unique talents and abilities no matter what is happening around them.

128

As the competition for results continues to heat up, only those hedge fund managers that stay centered and focused will excel. Put another way, those hedge fund managers who stay centered – in good and bad times – are the ones who will not only reach the financial pinnacle, but stay there.

A VERY STRESSFUL BUSINESS

Excelling in the hedge fund business calls for keeping your eye on making money – for that's what the business is undeniably all about. We've empirically found that success in the hedge fund business is predicated on:

➤➤ The special skills and talents of the hedge fund managers;

➤➤ A great deal of persistence and hard work; and

➤➤ A little bit of luck.

At the same time, the hedge fund business is ultra-stressful (Exhibit A.1). Based on our study of 294 financially successful hedge fund professionals with an average net worth of US$197.4 million, 79.3 percent found their job to be "very" stressful. Somewhat fewer, 67.3 percent, admitted that sometimes the stress of the business was a "little overwhelming." Moreover, 88.1 percent reported that they knew at least one very successful hedge fund professional who had suffered from "burnout."

EXHIBIT A.1:
A STRESSFUL BUSINESS FOR SUCCESSFUL
HEDGE FUND MANAGERS
N = 428 AFFLUENT INVESTORS

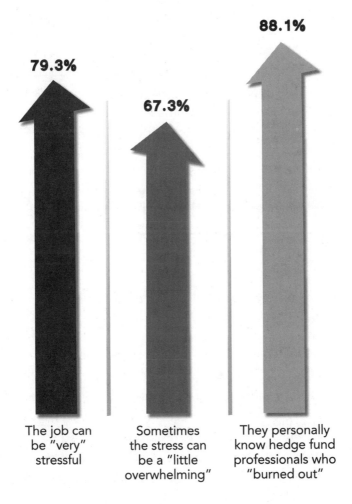

88.1%

79.3%

67.3%

| The job can be "very" stressful | Sometimes the stress can be a "little overwhelming" | They personally know hedge fund professionals who "burned out" |

129

THE
THREE D'S

It's a sad reality that some hedge fund managers become overwhelmed by the stresses of the business and fall to one of the "three D's" that are known to plague the industry: drink, drugs, and divorce.

However, some of the hedge fund professionals we studied employed successful strategies for handling the stress and the three D's. For example, some of them relied on "angst buffers," outside experts who understood what they were confronting and who provided the appropriate level and kind of support. Sometimes, other hedge fund professionals, including partners, can be good "angst buffers" so long as they don't create a vicious cycle that only makes matters worse by exacerbating anxiety.

For some hedge fund professionals, hiring business coaches is the best way to mitigate business stress. The key is for the business coaches to not be generic, working with a hedge fund manager one day and a senior executive at a manufacturing company the next, but to be truly and finely attuned to the world of the hedge fund professional.

STAYING
CENTERED

Industry research clearly demonstrates the need for hedge fund professionals to "stay centered." One hedge fund professional explained that when he was focused on doing what he did well, his fund followed suit. However, when he deviated from his expertise, which was currency trading, and tried to do "other things," such as expand into private equity through a side pocket, his fund's investment performance suffered, setting off a downward spiral.

We have found that the demise of many hedge funds – and the loss of the private wealth of the hedge fund professionals involved – is often a function of those professionals getting away from the very strengths that made them successful in the first place. What had enabled them to achieve extreme personal wealth was capitalizing on their often exceptional talents for investing. When hedge fund professionals are no longer centered on capitalizing on their unique abilities, they tend to make poor investment and business choices.

So what happens? How do these talented professional get so far off track?

In working with highly successful hedge fund professionals, we've heard a plethora of reasons for their having drifted off-center and squandered their unique abilities. Martha, for example, got all wrapped up in the internal politics of her three-person hedge fund. Instead, of concentrating on trading energy futures, her mind kept coming back to her conflicts with her partners. For over a year this went on and the performance of the hedge fund suffered significantly. With the resolution of these conflicts, the hedge fund was once again able to post exceedingly good returns. Sadly, however, given the strong personalities involved, it's quite common for partners in management companies to have issues that end up compromising their success, primarily because those issues distract the partners from exercising their unique abilities. The more expeditiously such matters are addressed, the more quickly the hedge fund can get back on track.

Simon was being "torn up" because his relatives, who also happened to be his investors, were giving him a hard time because his fund was down about 4 percent. As it happened, the fund had been up over 16 percent in each of the previous three years. Still, his relatives were dissatisfied and their constant

131

pressure and criticism were making his job of managing money more difficult. It became so nerve-racking that he even considered closing shop. By helping Simon get perspective and also helping him develop and implement a plan for dealing with his overbearing relatives, we were able to help him establish boundaries that provided him the breathing room he needed to concentrate on his special skills and talents. As a result, he bounced back with a vengeance, with his fund improving some 22 percent the next year.

What is clear is that when hedge fund professionals are distracted or deviating from their unique abilities, the results can be disastrous. On the other hand, by staying centered, hedge fund professionals are able to ride out difficult markets and mercurial investors, as well as their own (often) short-lived insecurities. Moreover, based on our research, those hedge fund professionals who stay centered on their unique abilities prove to be among the top ten percent of hedge fund professionals as measured by personal net worth.

CONCLUSIONS

For managers and investors alike, the hedge fund business is all about the money – and everyone knows it. But success in the business is predicated on long hours and considerable effort. Additionally, to succeed, hedge fund professionals must stay centered on their unique abilities. While some people looking at the business tend to only see the mansions and private jets, Patek Philippe watches, and free-flowing champagne, those rewards are predominantly a function of talent and a lot of hard work. Sustained success also requires a mindset that enables the winners to not only persevere in the face of adversity but handle success with aplomb, as the path is treacherous and the distractions are legion.

APPENDIX B:
WEALTH PRESERVATION

**With Richard J. Flynn, Partner-in-Charge of the
Rothstein Kass Family Office Group**

The hedge fund industry is about creating wealth. Through adroit investment management, the assets placed in hedge funds and funds-of-funds grow. As those assets grow, individual and institutional investors get wealthier and wealthier. Furthermore, the hedge fund professionals become wealthy as well.

Hedge fund professionals are generally so focused on creating wealth that they tend to neglect actions to efficiently transfer and protect that wealth. Thus, they need to turn to advanced planning specialists – the authorities on wealth preservation.

Just what is "wealth preservation?" Simply put:

> Wealth preservation is the process of safeguarding and potentially enhancing a hedge fund professional's net worth.

From whom or what do you need to safeguard your assets? In that regard, you need to be attentive to three broad categories:

▸ **TAX AUTHORITIES.** Governments the world over want their cut. Your objective, using bright-line transactions, is to give any taxing authority as little as legally permissible.

▸ **UNJUST LAWSUITS.** In a litigious society, significant private wealth can be decimated by unjust lawsuits brought by a variety of different people, from disgruntled partners, ex-spouses, and displeased investors to those who believe all hedge fund professionals are fabulously wealthy. The objective is to strongly discourage these overtures.

▸ UNEXPECTED CIRCUMSTANCES. The sudden death or disability of a partner in a management company can result in the disintegration of the hedge fund or fund-of-funds business and often take with it a sizeable portion of the partners' personal wealth. Your objective is to take the appropriate financial steps to mitigate the adverse effect of a partner's death or disability.

Operationally, wealth preservation is a critical process that regularly results in the repositioning and restructuring of your assets to preserve and sometimes increase your wealth. For hedge fund professionals, the wealth preservation process leverages tax laws and regulations, often employing tax-driven, cutting-edge strategies and sophisticated financial products in unique ways. At its simplest, wealth preservation can be conceptualized as involving two interrelated processes: estate planning and asset protection planning.

ESTATE
PLANNING

Deciding who should receive your hard earned wealth when you die is what estate planning is all about. Specifically:

> Estate planning is the process of legally structuring the future disposition of current and projected assets.

Every estate plan includes documents written to effectively dispose of the assets you own at death, usually a simple will and a revocable trust. Estate planning can also involve lifetime giving. This can be simple, such as making annual gifts to your children and grandchildren, or it can be quite complex, incorporating structures such as offshore captive insurance companies and special purpose entities. Finally, estate

134

planning can be accomplished by preventing assets from ever becoming part of your estate. For example, properly structured life insurance should never be included in your taxable estate. Similarly, freezing the value of your equity stake in your management company ensures that any future appreciation is not considered to be part of your estate.

Nearly all the 294 wealthy hedge fund professionals we surveyed, 91.8 percent, said they were concerned about properly providing for their loved ones when they died (Exhibit B.1). Still, only about three out of five of them had an estate plan that was more than a will (Exhibit B.2). That means that 121 of the hedge fund professionals we surveyed did not have an estate plan.

EXHIBIT B.1:
CONCERNED FOR THE WELL-BEING OF LOVED ONES
N = 294 WEALTHY HEDGE FUND PROFESSIONALS

135

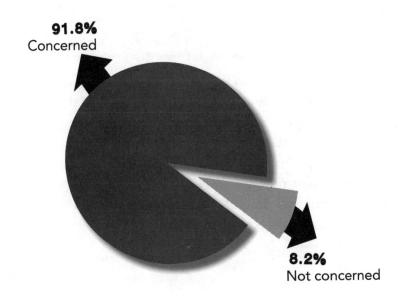

91.8%
Concerned

8.2%
Not concerned

EXHIBIT B.2:

HAVE AN ESTATE PLAN

N = 294 WEALTHY HEDGE FUND PROFESSIONALS

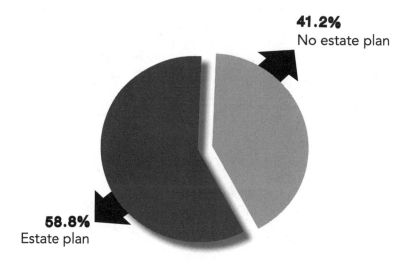

41.2%
No estate plan

58.8%
Estate plan

As to those hedge fund professionals who had estate plans, it was impossible to directly evaluate the quality of their plans, so we used proxies. By a number of measures, we found that nearly all the estate plans were outdated. For example, 91.9 percent of the hedge fund professionals who had estate plans were wealthier now then when they had crafted their estate plans (Exhibit B.3). In fact, in a substantial number of cases, the hedge fund professionals were wealthier by multiples.

EXHIBIT B.3:
WEALTHIER SINCE THE ESTATE PLAN
N = 172 WEALTHY HEDGE FUND PROFESSIONALS

91.9%
Wealthier

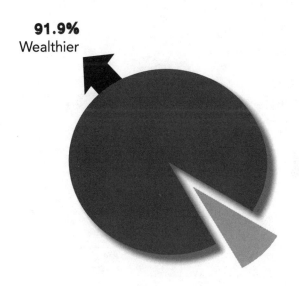

Another indication that most of these estate plans were outdated was the fact that 50.3 percent of the hedge fund professionals had experienced a major life-changing event since their plans were written (Exhibit B.4). Life-changing events included such landmark occurrences as a marriage, the birth of a child or grandchild, a divorce, or a death in the family.

EXHIBIT B.4:
EXPERIENCED A LIFE-CHANGING
EVENT SINCE THE ESTATE PLAN
N = 172 WEALTHY HEDGE FUND PROFESSIONALS

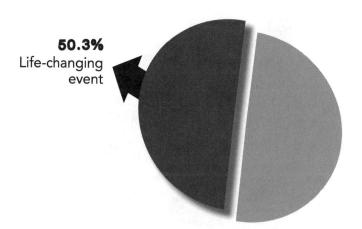

50.3%
Life-changing
event

138

In sum, while most hedge fund professionals have estate plans, it's highly likely that they are out of date, sometimes egregiously so. Whether this is because of changes in the tax code or life-changing events, these old estate plans are unlikely to accomplish the hedge fund professional's current goals and objectives.

Compounding the problem is the fact that most estate plans for the wealthy were not at the cutting edge – or even in the neighborhood – when they were written (let alone today). Consequently, because they had estate plans that were behind the curve when written and are now both outmoded and outdated, many hedge fund professionals are missing opportunities to preserve their wealth and may even be unnecessarily exposing their assets to risk.

ASSET PROTECTION PLANNING

We have found that many other hedge fund professionals are justifiably concerned about being victims of baseless lawsuits. The best form of defense is asset protection planning. Asset protection is simply another form of planning derived from other types of legal and risk management processes. A high-quality asset protection plan will integrate a variety of risk management products and leverage current laws to provide hedge fund professionals with a viable defense for their assets in case a party who has targeted their wealth confronts them with an unjust claim. In a nutshell:

Asset protection planning is the process of employing risk management products and legally acceptable strategies to ensure a person's wealth is not unjustly taken from him or her.

Because of the litigation lottery and similar structural malfunctions permeating our society, coupled with the general perception that all hedge fund professionals are extraordinarily rich, asset protection planning is a wise move for most – if not all – hedge fund professionals.

The objectives of asset protection planning are fairly simple:

- First, to mitigate the possibility of being sued by motivating a creditor to settle. In effect, a creditor and his or her attorneys will recognize the situation for what it is, and a lawsuit will be avoided or the settlement will be negotiated for pennies on the dollar.

- Second, in the case of a lawsuit, to minimize or even eliminate the financial effect of a judgment against the hedge fund professional. While a plaintiff may prevail in the lawsuit, the financial burden is greatly mitigated and many of the hedge fund professional's assets are simply, and legitimately, not available to satisfy the judgment.

Many hedge fund professionals think of, or are introduced to, asset protection planning only after they've been sued. As a result, a lawsuit decision against them or a messy divorce can destroy years of wealth creation. This is pertinent because 39.8 percent of the wealthy hedge fund professionals we surveyed had been involved in unjust lawsuits or divorce proceedings (Exhibit B.5). We also found that most hedge fund professionals understood the consequences of such situations as 83.3 percent of them were concerned about being involved in an unjust lawsuit or a divorce proceeding at some point (Exhibit B.6).

140

EXHIBIT B.5:

BEEN INVOLVED IN UNJUST LAWSUITS AND/
OR DIVORCE PROCEEDINGS
N = 294 WEALTHY HEDGE FUND PROFESSIONALS

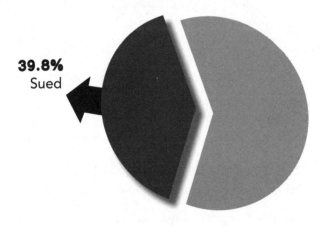

39.8%
Sued

EXHIBIT B.6:

CONCERNED ABOUT BEING INVOLVED IN UNJUST LAWSUITS AND/OR DIVORCE PROCEEDINGS
N = 294 WEALTHY HEDGE FUND PROFESSIONALS

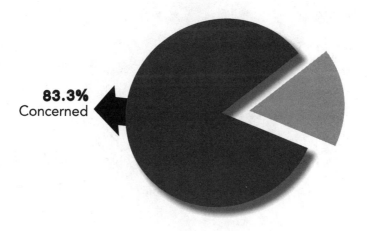

83.3%
Concerned

141

When working with hedge fund professionals, we often find them to have a vague yet powerful fear of being sued. The general perception is that a jury may not be very sympathetic because its members will see a hedge fund professional as filthy rich and easily able to absorb any loss. While the logic for establishing an asset protection plan is compelling, only 44.2 percent of the hedge fund professionals we surveyed had done so (Exhibit B.7).

EXHIBIT B.7:

# HAVE AN ASSET PROTECTION PLAN
N = 294 WEALTHY HEDGE FUND PROFESSIONALS

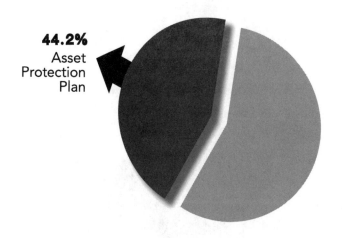

44.2%
Asset
Protection
Plan

The warped public perception of hedge fund managers' wealth, coupled with an "it's-not-my-fault" mindset, makes hedge fund professionals prime targets for unjust lawsuits. Considering the number of gold diggers, business creditors, jilted lovers, and unhappy investors out there, it's not surprising that hedge fund professionals are squarely in the lawsuit crosshairs.

The solution for combatting these scenarios is asset protection planning and it's wise for concerned hedge fund professionals to explore the options available to them. Regrettably, many of the professionals we surveyed did not have up-to-date asset protection plans. The cost of being unprepared can be painfully high, as those who've experienced it can attest.

CONCLUSIONS

Wealth preservation is the process of ensuring that hedge fund professionals keep their wealth or transfer it to the people and charitable institutions they choose. Successful hedge fund professionals are very busy people focused on creating wealth for themselves and other people and, as a consequence, many of them have failed to take the proper steps when it comes to estate and asset protection planning. Or, having taken those steps at one point, they have not updated their plans recently enough to reflect their increased net worth or to take advantage of the latest wealth preservation strategies. This is a situation that can be easily corrected – and should be, given both the assets and public perceptions in play.

INSTITUTIONAL INVESTORS

Aside from studying affluent investors who have invested in hedge funds, we have also surveyed institutional investors who have done so. In total, we researched 286 institutional investors, 67.1 percent of whom were involved with pension funds while the remaining 32.9 percent were foundations and non-profit organizations (Exhibit C.1). In total they had US$28.9 billion invested in hedge funds and funds-of-funds, the majority of which was invested by the pension funds (Exhibit C.2).

EXHIBIT C.1:

INSTITUTIONAL INVESTORS

N = 286 INSTITUTIONAL INVESTORS

145

67.1%
Pension funds

32.9%
Foundations
and non-profits

EXHIBIT C.2:
ASSETS INVESTED
N = 286 INSTITUTIONAL INVESTORS

$23.8B

$5.1B

Pension
funds

Foundations
and non-profits

146

SOURCING HEDGE FUNDS
AND FUNDS-OF-FUNDS

As the chart below illustrates (Exhibit C.3), almost three-quarters of the institutional investors we surveyed relied on their own networking and research efforts when sourcing funds. About two-thirds turned to investment management consultants while seminars and conferences were important to about one-third. Nearly one-quarter of the respondents found capital introductions professionals very useful.

EXHIBIT C.3:
SOURCING FUNDS
N = 286 INSTITUTIONAL INVESTORS

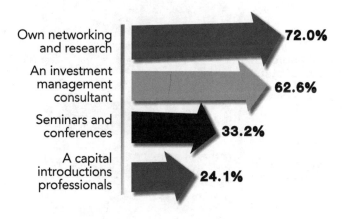

Own networking and research — **72.0%**

An investment management consultant — **62.6%**

Seminars and conferences — **33.2%**

A capital introductions professionals — **24.1%**

147

SELECTION
CRITERIA

A fund's track record was the most important criteria institutional investors used when deciding which firm to invest with, but the fund's investment strategy or approach was a very close second (Exhibit C.4). For about nine out of ten institutional investors surveyed, the hedge fund or fund-of-funds had to be appropriate to their overall investment portfolio. Nearly, two-thirds cited the way the fund managed risk as a major consideration, and 60.1 percent of the respondents said the quality of the vendors employed by the candidate firm was relevant. Slightly fewer were focused on the fund's fee structure.

EXHIBIT C.4:
SELECTION CRITERIA
N = 286 INSTITUTIONAL INVESTORS

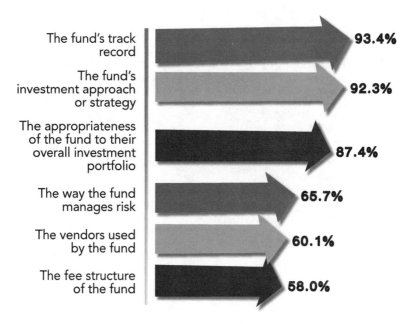

The fund's track record — **93.4%**

The fund's investment approach or strategy — **92.3%**

The appropriateness of the fund to their overall investment portfolio — **87.4%**

The way the fund manages risk — **65.7%**

The vendors used by the fund — **60.1%**

The fee structure of the fund — **58.0%**

148

SWITCHED FUNDS
IN THE PREVIOUS 12 MONTHS

Almost a quarter of the institutional investors we surveyed had switched out of a hedge fund or fund-of-funds in the preceding year (Exhibit C.5). The two principal reasons for switching, both cited by more than one-half of the respondents, were poor investment performance and the fact that the hedge fund professionals were unresponsive (Exhibit C.6).

EXHIBIT C.5:
SWITCHED FUNDS
N = 286 INSTITUTIONAL INVESTORS

22.0%
Previous 12 months

149

EXHIBIT C.6:
REASONS FOR SWITCHING
N = 63 INSTITUTIONAL INVESTORS

Poor investment
performance

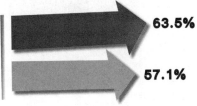 **63.5%**

The fund professionals
were unresponsive

57.1%

SATISFACTION
WITH PRIMARY HEDGE FUND
OR FUND-OF-FUNDS

Overall, only 57.1 percent of institutional investors were highly satisfied with their primary hedge fund or fund-of-funds (the fund with their largest allocation) (Exhibit C.7).

EXHIBIT C.7:
LEVELS OF OVERALL SATISFACTION
N = 286 INSTITUTIONAL INVESTORS

150

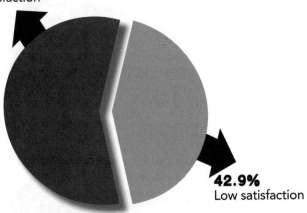

57.1%
High satisfaction

42.9%
Low satisfaction

CONCLUSIONS

While there are many similarities in the decision making processes between affluent investors and institutional investors, we can see by this brief set of highlights that there are also significant differences such as the percentages that are highly satisfied with their primary hedge fund or fund-of-funds. While the marketing approaches we recommend for affluent investors such as Storywork and creating a customized relationship management plan are valuable for institutional investors as well, they are essentially distinct types of investors with their own unique priorities and processes, and should be treated as such by appropriately modifying both the strategies and the implementation.

APPENDIX D:
HEDGE FUNDS, FUNDS-OF FUNDS, AND THE FAMILY OFFICE

Adapted from *Inside the Family Office: Managing the Fortunes of the Exceptionally Wealthy* by Russ Alan Prince and Hannah Shaw Grove, Wealth Management Press, Penton Media, 2004.

What we today refer to as family offices have their origins in the private investment companies of the 17th century. In Britain, for instance, the Office of the Exchequer – the royal family office – handled the king's affairs. At about the same time, the Rothschild family was expanding its family banking operation as the sons of Baron von Rothschild took up residence in London, Paris, Naples, Vienna, and Frankfurt. While each son engaged in banking activity, the father retained control of the family's investments. Over time, the Rothschild approach to aggregating and centralizing wealth management was adopted by European royalty as well as wealthy families without peerages.

It wasn't until the early 20th century, however, that the idea took firm hold in other parts of the world. The concentration of wealth in the hands of families such as the Carnegies, Rockefellers, and Pews led to the broad-based acceptance of the family office in the United States. Because of the costs involved, most wealthy families turned at first to trust companies to manage their affairs – what we would today define as a commercial family office. However, as the number of affluent families increased, the costs came down and the single and multi-family office gained currency, so to speak. Single and multi-family offices have since been established across the globe while the depth and breadth of services offered by financial institutions expanded, to keep pace with the demands of the ultra-affluent.

THE FAMILY OFFICE
TODAY

With a family office, the fortune of the exceptionally wealthy family is given a life of its own. Conceptually, the family office is the last word in providing financial coordination and management with a solid and sometimes nearly exclusive focus on the investments of the family. When a more holistic approach is taken, as is increasingly the case, the benefits for the family are realized through synergies, resulting in the maximizing of family assets in accord with the family's specific agenda. In effect, the essence of the family office is to ensure high customization and control over select financial affairs, especially the family's investment portfolio. The family office accomplishes this objective:

154

> ▸▸ By providing investment expertise itself and/or the careful screening, selection, and oversight of various investment managers and other professional advisors;

> ▸▸ By providing various administrative services such as investment recordkeeping; and

> ▸▸ By providing and overseeing additional services for the family and family members such as advanced planning and lifestyle services.

The driving rationale of every family office is that the family's assets are better managed by a single organization dedicated to, and capable of, catering to the group needs and wants of an exceptionally wealthy family (and, when appropriate, the needs and wants of individual family members). By having a detailed and comprehensive view of the family's financial picture, especially with respect to various tax issues, in conjunction with an ability to address a number of (and, in some cases, every) financial issue, the office is able to maximize the value of the family's assets and help it achieve its non-financial agenda, which may include such things as strategic philanthropy or family cohesion.

THE THREE TYPES
OF FAMILY OFFICES

In an effort to move beyond the unsubstantiated anecdotes and hearsay about family offices, we adopted a rigorous empirical approach. We conducted in-depth and structured interviews with the executive directors (or equivalent) of 92 single-family offices and 234 multi-family offices. We employed the same approach with the "heads" (their titles varied) of 327 commercial family offices.

Our first finding, as expected, was that the family office is a theme with many variations. But even with a great deal of variance in the family office universe, the following three basic business models dominated.

THE SINGLE-FAMILY OFFICE. The "classic" family office is one in which a single exceptionally wealthy family takes control of its finances by creating a coordinating organization for itself. Our study of family offices included 92 such offices with wealth ranging from US$281 million to US$1.6 billion. Their mean net-worth was US$772.6 million and their median net-worth US$601.4 million. Their investable assets ranged from US$197 million to US$843 million with a mean of US$696.2 million and a median of US$488.3 million. In the aggregate, we were looking at US$71.1 billion in net worth and US$64.1 billion in investable assets. In sum, these family offices (and the families they represent) were very comfortably situated at the financial apex.

THE MULTI-FAMILY OFFICE. The multi-family office is formed when 1) a single family office decides to add other families to extend its financial reach, or 2) when a number of families with similar goals get together at the outset to create the office and gain greater financial clout as well as greater influence over key aspects of their lives. For our purposes, to be defined as a multi-family office – and be distinguished from a commercial family office – there must be an "anchor" family that had at least 30 percent of the office's total capital. The net-worth of the multi-family offices in our study ranged from US$64 million to US$720 million. The mean net-worth of the multi-family offices was US$259.6 million, while the median net-worth was US$113.7 million. The investable assets ranged from US$49 million to US$514 million for each office, while the mean was US$106.2 million and the median was US$74.3 million.

THE COMMERCIAL FAMILY OFFICE. The commercial family office is a multi-family office without an anchor family. An array of professional advisors including private bankers, accountants, brokers, and investment managers have set themselves up as commercial family offices, as have some of the nation's larger financial services firms. The clients of commercial family offices tended to be less affluent than those in both the single-family and multi-family offices. Their net-worth ranged from US$13 million to US$812 million with a mean net-worth of US$53.2 million and a median net-worth of US$19.8 million. As for investable assets, the range was from US$13 million to US$481 million with a mean of US$31.9 million and a median of US$17.5 million.

FAMILY OFFICES
AND THE USE OF HEDGE
FUNDS AND FUNDS-OF-FUNDS

In the previous two years, nearly all the 653 family offices we surveyed had sourced hedge funds (Exhibit D.1). More commercial family offices, 92.0 percent, had done so, compared to multi-family offices (81.6 percent), and single-family offices (78.3 percent), but the interest and involvement at every level was strong.

About half of the family offices had used an outside funds-of-funds, a percentage skewed by the fact that 88.4 percent of commercial family offices had done so, compared to less than 20 percent of the other family office types. This is a function of commercial family offices tending to have more, albeit "less wealthy," clients, and to provide a larger number of investment options.

EXHIBIT D.1:

EMPLOYING EXTERNAL HEDGE FUNDS AND FUNDS-OF-FUNDS
N = 653 FAMILY OFFICES

INVESTMENT	SINGLE-FAMILY OFFICE	MULTI-FAMILY OFFICE	COMMERCIAL FAMILY OFFICE	TOTAL
Hedge funds	78.3%	81.6%	92.0%	86.4%
Funds-of-funds	13.0%	18.8%	88.4%	52.8%

157

CONCLUSION

From managing a fund-of-funds to using select hedge funds to round out an asset allocation plan, family offices have made considerable use of external hedge fund managers. It's very clear that family offices will continue to tap into outside talent when it comes to these alternative investments, in large part because it's difficult to bring the requisite level of talent in-house.

SCENES FROM THE FRINGE

Adapted from *After the Facts* by Russ Alan Prince
Private Wealth: Advising the Exceptionally Affluent,
August/September 2007 Issue.

Having consulted to the super-rich for nearly two decades now, we've witnessed things from the ridiculous to the sublime, and one of the most interesting subgroups – which never fails to surprise and fascinate – is known simply as the "Fringe."

Lest you think the Fringe is a euphemism for a group of dysfunctional outsiders, it's not. Our experience with the Fringe has been principally through what can best be described as global family office structures. They are large, private, and tightly controlled. They want to grow through investment performance and alliances with like-minded organizations. They prefer to conduct business and source deals with known entities that have passed through extraordinary security and background checks. For the most part, members of these family offices are well-regarded, super-successful individuals and families that control enormous amounts of wealth and are active in their local and international communities. And, like most extremely wealthy people, they value discretion in their personal and professional relationships. This emphasis on privacy and exclusivity means both the offices and their clients are, by design, very much outside of the mainstream.

But operating out of the spotlight is just the tip of the iceberg for the Fringe. One other attribute that distinguishes the Fringe from more conventional family offices and private wealth organizations is the overriding eroticism and decadence that permeates the corporate culture. Additionally, the executives in the organizations and the member families share a degree of personal moral flexibility that adds a layer of pleasure to their relationships.

One organization that squarely fits the definition of Fringe controls roughly US$20 billion with "headquarters" in Hong Kong. From its female chief executive on down through the female-dominated management ranks, there is a fundamental belief in the principles, techniques, training, and use of tantric sex. Another example of their focus on eroticism is a defining membership experience called the Play of Seven Knives. This is an esoteric "treatment" administered by a professional known as an "Adept" in seven stages over the course of several months – to the tune of about US$2 million. The treatments include a unique combination of baths, massages, potions, and knives that are hand-crafted just for this purpose; the unremitting prospect of being cut adds intensity and prompts an array of enthusiastic responses from those who experience it.

Another family office that can be considered part of the Fringe is based in England and oversees more than US$17 billion in assets. Their primary claim to Fringe status is an annual member event cryptically referred to as "The Gathering." The location of the affair rotates among the organization's real estate holdings, including castles and villas across the European continent. To ensure privacy and confidentiality, attendance is strictly controlled through a formal invitation process, a thorough investigation conducted in advance on all guests, and the use of biometric identification systems. The Gathering is a highly anticipated event for the super-affluent members and their friends of this family office and always has superb world cuisine, vintage wines and spirits, and performers such as acrobats and dancers throughout the grounds. The only requirement is that guests wear masks – and many choose to wear nothing else – and feel free to observe, participate, explore, or experiment with other receptive guests, with the toys and games provided by the staff, in orgiastic group activities, and in the many impromptu performances that occur over the multi-day event.

The Fringe exemplifies the secret worlds that are occupied by those at the pinnacle of the financial pyramid. For them, this is an insular environment – created and fed by serious money – where they can play hard and fast and the "rules of conduct" are flexible. In this world, the inhabitants have more in common than their socioeconomic status; they connect on a sensual, sexual level that allows them to coordinate their extensive financial resources and personal connections for their own amusement and enhancement.

ABOUT
THE AUTHORS

RUSS ALAN PRINCE is the world's leading authority on private wealth, the author of 40 books on the topic, and a highly-sought counselor to individuals and families with significant global resources, and their advisors.
www.russalanprince.com
russ@russalanprince.com

HANNAH SHAW GROVE is a widely recognized author, columnist, coach, consultant, and speaker, and an expert on the mindset, behaviors, concerns, preferences, and finances of high-net-worth individuals.
www.hsgrove.com
hannah@hsgrove.com

ABOUT
THE SPONSOR

Rothstein Kass provides audit, tax, accounting and consulting services to hedge funds, funds-of-funds, private equity funds, broker-dealers and registered investment advisors. The firm is recognized nationally as a top service provider to the industry through its Financial Services Group. The Financial Services Group consults on a wide range of organizational, operational and regulatory issues. The firm also advises on fund structure, both inside and outside the U.S., compliance and financial reporting, as well as tax issues from a federal, state, local and international compliance perspective.

Rothstein Kass   Rothstein Kass has offices in New York, New Jersey, California, Colorado, Texas and the Cayman Islands. More information is available at www.rkco.com.

ABOUT
THE PUBLISHER

Elite Traveler is the world's leading luxury lifestyle publication. With BPA-audited distribution aboard private jets and mega-yachts and through other high-end venues in over 90 countries, it is designed specifically for a super-affluent, global readership that includes owners of significant businesses, C-Level executives at multi-national corporations, athletes, entertainers, royalty, government leaders and their families.

Reaching more than 575,000 readers with each issue, *Elite Traveler's* unique editorial is specifically targeted to the private jet lifestyle, and delivers detailed coverage in key categories such as watches, jewelry, fashion, automotive, real estate and travel. *Elite Traveler* is an indispensable personal assistant for the ultra-wealthy in their quest for the best in supreme luxury products and services.

165

THE PRIVATE JET LIFESTYLE MAGAZINE

Elite Traveler is part of Universal Media, a global communications and publishing firm. More information is available at www.elitetraveler.com.